Macrobiotic Miracle

Macrobiotic Miracle

How a Vermont Family
Overcame Cancer

By Virginia Brown *with* Susan Stayman

Japan Publications, Inc.

Note to the reader: This book is not a substitute for professional
medical care. It is essential that any reader who has a serious illness
consult with their physician before implementing the approach to
health outlined in this book.

Published by JAPAN PUBLICATIONS, INC., Tokyo & New York

Distributors:
UNITED STATES: *Kodansha International/USA, Ltd., through Harper &
Row, Publishers, Inc., 10 East 53rd Street, New York, N. Y. 10022.*
SOUTH AMERICA: *Harper & Row, Publishers, Inc., International Depart-
ment.* CANADA: *Fitzhenry & Whiteside Ltd., 150 Lesmill Road, Don
Mills, Ontario M3B 2T6.* MEXICO & CENTRAL AMERICA: *HARLA S. A.
de C. V. Apartado 30–546, Mexico 4, D. F.* BRITISH ISLES: *International
Book Distributors Ltd., 66 Wood Lane End, Hemel Hempstead, Herts
HP2 4RG.* EUROPEAN CONTINENT: *Fleetbooks, S. A., c/o Feffer and Simons
(Nederland) B. V., Rijnkade 170, 1382 GT Weesp, The Netherlands.*
AUSTRALIA & NEW ZEALAND: *Bookwise International, 1 Jeanes Street,
Beverley, South Australia 5007.* THE FAR EAST & JAPAN: *Japan Publications
Trading Co., Ltd., 1–2–1, Sarugaku-cho, Chiyoda-ku, Tokyo 101.*

First edition: December 1984

LCCC No. 84–080645
ISBN 0-87040-573-X

Printed in U.S.A.

Acknowledgment

The authors wish to thank Frank Brown, Edward and Wendy Esko, Michio and Aveline Kushi, and Bennett and June Stayman for their continuing support and inspiration.

To my mother
Adelaide Marion Bratt
from whom my love of nature and strength came

Awareness

Awareness is seeing with your heart—hearing sound in
stillness—finding color in gray—violet—blue—green
and sometimes gold—catching your breath at tenderness
—a baby's smile—a loving glance—looking and wondering at the moon and stars—feeling the warmth of the
sun—soft petals of flowers—watching a robin hopping
or a plant opening its leaves—sparkling water or driving
rain—softly falling snow—dark branches against a winter
sky—light of early morning.

Knowing love and giving of it.

Conscious of life—every moment.

ADELAIDE M. BRATT

Preface

THE CHURCH was especially beautiful that certain day in May of 1947, at twilight, with a candle at every pew and, on the altar masses of dogwood in bloom, with more candle-light shining like tiny stars between. My brother, Chuckie, was waiting with me, listening to our sister Marion's husband Fred sing so beautifully (*Through the Years*, which Jinny and I loved and still love so much). The song ended, and our married life was about to begin—my Jinny, all in white coming down the aisle on the arm of her papa.

We had met so many years before—I was sixteen, living in Connecticut with my family; Jinny was fifteen, living in Massachusetts with hers—Depression years, hard years but good years.

Having been invited by a friend of mine to share a vacation at a lake in New Hampshire with his family and him, I met Jinny, there with her family. We had a very enjoyable time, but then it was back to Connecticut and school.

The years passed very swiftly, Pearl Harbor Day arrived, and on my twenty-first birthday I enlisted in the army and was sent to Fort Devens to be inducted. Not being far from Winchester, Massachusetts, where Jinny lived, also not having written or heard from her since our time at the lake, I sent her a penny postcard asking if I could call and see her. But, the way the army works, even before I received a reply, I was sent to Virginia for my basic training—but we did begin a beautiful correspondence. Fate and circumstances prevented us from seeing each other however; before long I was in North Africa fighting a war, and after that, in England. In the meantime Jinny had finished her nurse's training and had enlisted in the Army Nurse Corps.

Finally the war in Europe was over. Once home I found out that Jinny was on a boat going to Japan and the Philippines. Another year went by—lots and lots of letters, pictures, and prayers. Finally, after not seeing each other for nine years, the day arrived, and I am sure we both knew it was meant to be.

Our married life has been and is a beautiful one—full of loving, sharing good and bad, hard and easy, growing older and wiser each year and, I guess, learning more about each other all the while. I know Jinny never ceases to amaze me with her ability to reach out to others in their time of need, and in her broad and beautiful belief in God and all His wonders. And, of course, at times her stubborness—her willingness to discuss a subject at great length to win her point.

As for her being stubborn and daring, a nurse friend who was with her in the army told me how, when their hospital ship arrived in Manila Harbor at night, someone dared Jinny to jump off the top deck into the water—which, like a fool, she did. Or, the other extreme, which was during the first year we were married, she insisted on having my sister, Grace, who was born with cerebral palsy and confined to bed and chair up to that point in her life, to our house in Massachusetts, where Jinny went to work and convinced Grace she could become nearly independent. Before long Grace could get from her wheelchair into bed and out, and could use the bathroom, cook meals for herself. Her new independence enabled Grace to go to college and in her own beautiful way to touch the lives of so many people. Until the day Grace died, she and Jinny never stopped their arguing and discussing everything from outer space to each and every thing along the way.

This is just a small bit about my Jinny, whom I love very dearly, and I very prayerfully thank so many people who helped us to a macrobiotic way of life when Jinny was so ill. I am firmly convinced after seeing her come back, one could say almost from the dead—that her strong belief in God, her very special stubborness, her diet and exercise, and the loving support of our beautiful family did indeed bring my Jinny back to me so we can, together, fulfill what was meant to be our destiny.

FRANK BROWN
Boston, 1984

The Long, Slow Climb

WE THINK OF IT as a slow and trudging journey through the valley of winter, but in reality it is a long and steady climb up the cold slope toward spring. Now we face both the best and the worst of the year's dark season, long nights, short days, brilliant starlight, a distant sun, and inevitable change.

HAL BORLAND
from *Twelve Moons of the Year*

1

I'd like to know
what this whole show
is all about
before it's out.
—Piet Hein

O<small>N</small> T<small>UESDAY</small>, A<small>UGUST</small> 22, 1978 my daughter, Melissa, drove me to the Burlington Medical Center in Burlington, Vermont, where I underwent surgical removal of a mole on the upper part of my left arm. No bigger than a dime, that mole was actually huge in its implications affecting my future.

Melissa, my youngest child and a senior in high school at the time, waited outside while I lay on my stomach on the operating table. The doctor dug deeply into my arm. An anesthetic had been given, but it didn't seem to matter. The more deeply he cut into my arm, the more he seemed to bore into something unknown. I shut my eyes tightly, determined not to cry out.

All of a sudden the operating room was filled with the sound of the telephone ringing. One of the nurses answered it. She rushed back and grabbed my other arm. The results of the biopsy, taken a few days earlier, were very bad.

"Malignant melanoma, stage IV," she said and, squeezing my arm, she asked me, "Do you know what that means?"

Of course I did. I had been a registered nurse for thirty-five years.

Melanoma is a form of skin cancer. At its fourth stage it has spread internally to the organs and is considered terminal.

I had perhaps six months to live.

I received this news lying on my stomach, about halfway through the operation. The doctor continued to remove the mole. The operating room was chilly and quiet. The nurse's words clapped the air and floated gently to the bare floor, hovering, finally piling up at the edge of the table where I lay, just below my nose. Cancer . . . Malignant . . . Death . . . What sort of broom could sweep this mess away?

As he sewed me up, the doctor broke his silence by asking, "Why did you wait so long?" When I said nothing, he added, "You must have known something was wrong. It takes years —at least two—for this to become so severe." He was, I think, disappointed in the way I was handling my own case. After all, what sort of nurse, what kind of a professional would let this go untreated for so long?

The truth is, I hadn't wanted to face it, didn't want to face it now. I knew there was something terribly wrong, but I didn't want to deal with it. I was like a person who had refused to hear the question, couldn't hear it because of the cotton I had figuratively put in my ears. I was beginning to realize that when things happen to you, yourself, they are a lot harder to see, harder to focus on. I remained silent, for I really had no answer to the doctor's question . . . .

* * *

Outside in the waiting room, Melissa cried when I told her I had cancer. During the thirty minute drive back home as she kept her eyes focused on the road, I was reminded of when she was first learning to drive. For some reason I remember trying to see the individual leaves on the trees. I felt that if I could just see one whole perfect little leaf, all would be well. But we were traveling too fast.

I slid down in the seat and laid my head back. Thoughts ran through me. What would I do? What would happen? Would I live anyway, in spite of what the doctor had told me

—that I had only a few months to live? Is it possible that he was wrong? I felt so sick, it was more probable that he was correct—that I was in fact right now in the process of dying of cancer. I ran my fingertips over the skirt of my dress, smoothing the wrinkles. I couldn't believe that I wouldn't grow old! I shook my head from side to side as if to jiggle the contents, as if to rearrange things so they'd look better. I searched my mind for something, *anything*, that would offer comfort. I felt that the answer was there amid all the thoughts, ideas, experiences, memories and hopes, but I just couldn't lay a finger on it.

When I was a little girl, we went to the shore in Maine once and, walking along the beach, I had wanted to collect all the shells I could. There were quite a few along the water's edge, but they were mostly broken. I would pick up the fragments and admire them—although ragged and incomplete, there was usually something about each of them that was interesting to me. But Mama had said, "Just take one, Jinny." One shell. So I picked up the colorful fragments and laid them down again. Then, backing up a way from the water, I began to sift through the sand with my fingers. To my delight I found more shells, some were whole. During the week by the ocean I spent most of my time searching through the sand for just the right shell. The fair skin on my shoulders and neck got very burned, and Mama rubbed cream there while my sister Tarny watched. When it was time to leave and we were packed into the car, I took the shell I had chosen from my pocket and turned it over in my hands. I hoped fervently that it was the *right* shell. I didn't know when I'd ever come back to the shore again, and I wanted to have the best shell to remember it by. I felt a sense of dissatisfaction though, as I looked at it, because although it was very beautiful, I was certain that if I went back to the beach tomorrow or the next day or the day after, I would find an even better one.

This was the same feeling I had as I returned again and again to the far corners of my head, turning over, as it were, the fertile topsoil of my mind, trying to uncover something that would ease my fear and tell me what I should do. Like the shell, I longed for something to grasp in my hand that would offer instant recollection of the elusive key that unlocks the door to our memory of ourselves when young, when carefree on holiday at the beach, when filled with the power and well-being of health. If I could only find the door and insert the key—and go in. Everywhere, doors were shutting in my face. Never before had my own abilities failed me. My life for the past thirty-five years had been filled with the joys and problems of nursing, raising six children, and helping my husband with his business, as we carved our life out of the rough stone of rural Vermont. I had always relied on the fact that no matter what happened, I could always find a solution. Now, however, the layers of accumulated experience were resisting my desperate scrutiny, thereby leaving me outside— alone and very afraid.

My husband Frank was in the yard digging up an old tree stump when we got home. He could tell by my face that things had gone badly at the hospital. When I told him that I had malignant melanoma, stage IV, he looked at me very carefully, taking in what I had said. He asked me to repeat what I had said. He waited for me to add something that would soften the gravity of what I was telling him, but all I could do was look back at him. Then he turned and headed for the woods at the end of the yard, where I knew he would walk until he was ready to come home.

I looked after him as I had so many times during our married life when he turned his back on our house, our children, problems, cares and difficulties for a few minutes each day and went into the woods alone to walk. There he found something he could get nowhere else. Renewed and refreshed, he always came back to us ready to shingle a roof or listen to his small son's description of a dying bird. He drew strength from the dark woody forest and gave it back to us. I admired this very much.

Inside the house, Melissa threw her arms around me and cried. She held me around the neck. I felt the full weight of her love—not the joy of it, not the mother's pride, just the dead weight of it. I felt as though I would fall from the strain of it. I knew that if I died I would be failing my children and my husband.

I felt weak and Melissa helped me to sit down. Normally I weigh about one hundred thirty pounds, but since I had not been able to eat for a few months, my weight was down to under one hundred pounds.

Up to this point I had been used to full, active days at the hospital, at home raising our children and helping Frank. Now I had to content myself with gazing out the window. Sometimes I even got tired doing that.

I could no longer fulfill my responsibilities around the house. I was conscious of the fact that other people were covering for me. My daughters-in-law, Julie and Mary, were no longer just breezing in and out of our house to talk—they were "fixing things up a little," as Julie kindly put it. She and our son Jeffrey were living next door, and they came over a lot. Their older son Nathan had been born the previous December. I liked the way Jeffrey put the baby in a sling on his back and took him for a walk every morning. Julie would burst through the door to our house full of energy, bubbling with stories about Nathan while she ran a mop over the floors, dusted, straightened beds and washed the dishes in the sink. Even my thoughts couldn't keep up with her. It seemed she was moving faster than I could think. Ordinarily I would accomplish these household chores in about an hour, before helping Frank with the painting, wiring, plumbing, and shingling.

Now, however, I had all I could do to watch Julie run through the housework. I sat and watched or stared out the window. Julie has told me since that she just assumed I was exhausted and overwrought from our experience with the community we had been trying to build in northern Vermont on Lake Champlain, and which had recently failed, leaving Frank and me very heavily in debt. This community, called Kingsland Bay, did in fact use up our strength and financial resources, but there was something else that was eating away at my vitality—a sickness deep within of which I was only partly aware, because that was all I wanted to know. Jeffrey's view, having been a quiet boy growing up in our noisy, active family, was that after thirty years of cooking, cleaning, nursing, and raising a family, I had become numb to it all and needed a rest. "Wouldn't *you* be sick and tired of clothes draped over chairs, dishes in the sink, and an endless chain of household chores to be done day in and day out?" he would ask anyone who addressed an accusatory remark to me. His explanation for my apparent laziness was acceptable to most of the members of our family, and I, too, believed it as a way of ignoring the real cause which was creeping through my blood and lodging in my bones. Had I taken an unhurried look at what was happening, I would have realized that this was not *me* they were talking about. I *liked* to work—any kind of work be it housework, construction, nursing, or whatever. My need to be busy was extreme and almost to the point of being a fault. So how had I all of a sudden turned into an old lady sitting in her kitchen letting her children take care of her? That question was to be answered slowly over the next year and a half, as I learned how to rid myself of the strangeness inside that was causing me to lose my love of life.

Mary came over a lot, too, and cleaned house. She and our youngest son Dexter were living a few minutes away. She had a soft way about her that calmed and soothed me during that time. She and Dexter had a recording studio in their house. I had just assisted in the home birth of their first child, Ki. I remember feeling exhausted by the experience, rather than exhuberant. Of course I was happy, but my energy was so low I couldn't partake fully of the joy and pride everyone else in the family was feeling. Having lost the ability to feel the highs and the lows, I was just barely getting along—hardly living at all.

I had become progressively weaker during the past two years, and my family had adapted and grown used to my inability to cope with the basics of daily living. For the most part they babied me and the days passed as always, without interruption. It is incredible, even to me, that I let myself get so rundown without doing anything about it. Yet I justify my negligence by saying that we were so involved with closing down the Kingsland Bay community that we didn't stop to look at ourselves. We were so caught up in our financial problems we didn't stop long enough to say, "Wait a minute, what's happening here?" It was as if we were desperately treading water, trying to keep our noses above the surface in order to breathe, ignoring all the while the shark that was circling our feet.

When Frank came through the kitchen door, he saw me in the living room and came to sit by me. He looked so awful I wanted to tell him it was all a mistake, that I didn't have cancer and that I wasn't going to die. The most important thing to me at that moment was to wipe the pain off his face.

Frank took my hand and held it in both of his. "What did the doctor say?" he asked.

I told him the doctor had wanted to know why I had waited so long before coming to see him, implying that I might have been cured, had I come earlier. Frank had heard me talk about cancer patients enough in the past to know what the prognosis was. I said, "I think he felt I knew what the diagnosis meant."

"What *does* it mean, Jinny?" Frank asked me quietly.

"Well, I suppose it means I'm going to die, Frank. That's the medical view anyway." I was cross that we were having this conversation, cross that I was sick, cross that Frank was upset about me, added to his monumental business problems. Just cross, I guess, that I was me, making all this trouble for everyone.

Frank went over to the window. Whenever he looks out a

window, he seems to reach for the best part in all the sky.

I was ashamed of how I was treating him. I'm afraid I was blaming him for my illness—for the neglect which had caused us to wait so long before seeing a doctor. It's not as if I had had no experience with cancer and didn't recognize the signs. I knew them all too well. They were a part of my daily life, caring for people—other people's mothers and wives—who had cancer. But when it came to my own illness, I had refused to accept it, had purposely ignored the signs. I now knew how people felt when they or a loved one had cancer. But there was a significant difference; I knew a lot about the treatment for cancer—surgery, radiation, and chemotherapy. I realized that I was more afraid of the treatment for cancer than I was of the disease itself.

We sat there in silence for a few minutes, and then I told Frank I was going to Amherst. He knew I had made arrangements to attend a macrobiotic[1] health seminar in Amherst, Massachusetts, at the urging of our oldest son David and his wife Deborah. It was a coincidence that the conference was scheduled to begin the day after I received the results of the biopsy.

"But you'd have to leave today," Frank said, getting up and stuffing his hands in his pockets. Something in the way he said it made me realize how afraid he was of losing me.

Maybe it *was* too much for me. Yet I knew that if I didn't make the effort to go, didn't find that will to push myself, that perhaps I wouldn't have the strength to get well, either. "Frank," I said, "my alternative is to have my lymph nodes removed and start chemotherapy." I looked at him. "And I don't want to die like that." And I didn't. I had decided that lying on the operating table earlier that day, when they had said, "malignant melanoma." I certainly *did* know what that meant. To the people in that operating room it meant that I would struggle against it with the arms they provided, including surgery, drugs, and radiation and that I would probably die, sooner or later. My life would be prolonged, perhaps, but what would the quality of that life be? I didn't want to find out. To me, the words malignant melanoma, spoken by the nurse in the operating room, meant something quite different. They meant I needed an alternative.

For years I had professed alternatives. In my heart I knew there must be another way to deal with serious illness. I believed that if we could just reach deep within ourselves, we could draw out the answer and humbly, carefully, faithfully, be rid of our miseries.

I had read the great religious books—the Koran, the Bible, works of the American Indians, and many others, searching for an answer to why we seem to suffer so much. I found much the same thing in all these works—a belief in an order that exists everywhere, that is not based on man-made reality, but rather on universal principles of harmony.

I had also read about the life of Edgar Cayce[2] in his biography entitled, *There Is A River*, written by Thomas Sugrue. I remember sitting on our couch reading about what this incredible man had done. Initially, I was fascinated by his extraordinary abilities, particularly the clairvoyant readings he did for people with serious health problems.

Furiously turning the pages of the book, I read about the remarkable things he had done. Here was something that made sense to me, in its own irrational, incredible way. I felt the authenticity of Mr. Cayce's clairvoyance and found myself believing wholeheartedly in the reality of a dimension which exists beyond the boundaries of our imaginations. I was fascinated.

Then, Thomas Sugrue reveals a very interesting twist in Mr. Cayce's life. After he had been doing readings for some time, helping people with specific physical problems, Cayce began delving deeper into the people he saw, beyond the physical breakdown of their bodies and into the mysterious background of their present lives. I stared at the word reincarnation looking up at me from the page. "That's it!" I jumped up off the couch and shook the book. I settled back again to read more about the concept that had been lurking in the back of my mind for such a long time, but which I had never before heard expressed.

The idea is that each life which a person experiences is a spiritual continuation of the last. While the temporal aspects such as parents, appearance, sex, environment, and financial situation may appear to be different from a previous life, a person, nonetheless, is carrying with him the effects of former lives. This supports the belief that everything that happens to us is, for some reason, necessary. The important thing is how we meet the challenges and choices in our lives, as they will influence us throughout eternity.

This book on the life of Edgar Cayce pointed the way for me into areas of thought I had never before explored. I read everything I could about him and about clairvoyance and that which is not readily explainable in scientific terms. As a medical professional, I may seem odd to some for having this perspective. But I did. And with good reason. At the hospital we see plenty of things we can't explain—at least not completely. I believe in medicine as a system, but I was coming to see it as only a part of the story in treating a person who is ill. The studies I made of Cayce's ideas and those of others tended to fill in the annoying gaps I felt in the world around me. We people, living in our modern age, lack the courage and conviction and the understanding that comes with a deep comprehension of the ways of nature. All traditional peoples have sought to explain seemingly arbitrary and unfair happenings in their lives by applying different philosophies, religions, and superstitions to them. I relaxed into the concept of our all having had past lives. It worked for me. It seemed *right*. And when it came time for me, during the course of my cancer, to grapple with other seemingly difficult questions like, "Why me?" there was a way for me to see beyond the short vision of my own present situation and to strive for a broader perspective. I felt liberated from a man-made world and sensed a freedom I had never known before. I was standing high on my toes, peeking over a fence into a whole, larger world.

But for the present time, I was very much caught up in the pain and troubles of my terminal cancer. The studies I had made of Edgar Cayce and others were there in the background, ready to support me later, but for now I was existing in a haze, unsure about what I should do.

A few years before, our son David and his wife Deborah discovered macrobiotics when they were considering what to do about their daughter's heart ailment. Their daughter Jessica, who was about a year old at that time, responded well to the change in her diet, which had been specially adapted to her infant needs. Within two years, she was perfectly healthy, and she and her parents continued on the diet. They said they liked the other effects that eating this way had on them. They would often talk to me about macrobiotics, but I only half listened. I was grateful for its apparent beneficial effect on my granddaughter, but hardly even tried the rice and vegetable dishes that Deborah and David brought with them to family parties.

During the past year, David and Deborah's efforts to interest me in macrobiotics became more intense. Perhaps they suspected that I had cancer; I don't know, we never discussed it. Although David often told me how bad I looked, I just thought he was being critical, which is sometimes his tendency. I had tucked macrobiotics into the back of my mind —far enough away that I didn't have to do it, but close enough that I could find it if I needed it, for I felt I *would* need it someday.

A few months before I had the biopsy, Deborah succeeded in talking me into attending this seminar in Amherst, sponsored by the East West Foundation[3]. David had said at the time, "Mother, do it. But *don't wait*, start today." How many times had he said this to me? He explained once again why I needed to eat brown rice and vegetables; organic, clean, healthy food that would make me whole and healthy. I don't know if he would say he knew I was terminally ill. He did know that I needed to change.

* * *

About a year before I had the mole on my arm biopsied—it was summertime—David came into the kitchen of the restaurant at the Kingsland Bay community where Julie and I were preparing dinner for the restaurant guests. David and Deborah were not living at the community, but they had come up to visit and Deb was helping us in the kitchen. It was six o'clock, we were already open, and I hadn't started the soup yet. The dried peas lay waiting in the pan, and I was cutting carrots as fast as I could.

My back was to the door, but I became aware of someone standing there, watching me. I knew it was David. I could feel his eyes on me. I was trying to concentrate on what I was doing so I wouldn't cut myself. He shifted a little and continued to stand there in the doorway. He had always done this. He would just stand there and stare, appraising everything. He was so maddening. What gave him the right?

"You look awful, Mother," he said softly. I kept cutting the carrots, wondering about a mother's love for her children. My hand slipped, causing the knife to graze my fingernail. David is so difficult to understand. Why does he say these things to me? "You can't keep on like this, Mother . . . ." he began again.

"What would you like me to do, dear," I swung around to face him, "throw the carrots into the pot whole?"

"No," he said, "you could take a look in the mirror once in a while and see how sick you look."

"*David!*" Julie looked up from the stove where she was stirring the pots. "David, stop it!" she said, going over to where he was standing in the doorway and faced him, hands on her hips.

He ignored her and continued, "You're skinny as a rail, and

you're always sitting down to rest. I saw you this afternoon. You sat down over there." He pointed to a table beyond the partition around the kitchen.

"*David!*" his wife Debbie shouted from the big sink where she was washing pots and pans.

He continued, "You were sitting with your head in your hands."

I put my knife down and looked at him. "So you think I'm sick because I'm tired. You don't think maybe running this place has anything to do with it!" I looked around the large kitchen which was sizzling and bubbling with dinner preparations.

"No." David turned and walked away.

"I just don't understand him sometimes," Deborah said as she came over and put her hand on my arm. Julie was still standing in the empty doorway with her hands on her hips, shaking her head. I could tell she was torn between saying what was on her mind and her desire to protect her sister-in-law.

"It's just his way," I told them. "He'll go and have a beer and cool off. He won't even remember."

We all knew that wasn't true. But there was a lot to do.

I dumped the carrots into the pot and started the onions. I was so tired. "Do you think anyone would notice if there weren't any onions in the soup?" I asked.

"No, Mother," Julie said, extending her arm and whisking the whole, untouched onions off the cutting board and back into the storage bin. "It's *enough*," she said firmly, as if she were commenting on everything. "The soup will be very good the way it is." She picked up the soup kettle and set it on the stove.

As I sat by the stove, stirring the pots, I wondered at how tired I was. I had put in a full day but not an unusually busy one. Why did I feel as if I might sink through the stool I was sitting on, through the floor, into the earth and on below to whatever was there? Maybe David had a point . . . .

That wasn't an isolated instance. David was always telling me how sick I looked and that I should eat brown rice. This made the rest of the family very angry, and they were always telling him to be quiet. They thought he was a trouble maker and that he was being overly critical. I wanted to believe everyone else because it shielded me from having to face up to the possibility that I might really be sick. I also couldn't stand a lot of fuss. I didn't want to see my family upset about me. So I buried whatever feelings I had that there might be something seriously wrong with me in order to preserve the harmony and closeness of my family, which to me is so very important.

I did, however, begin to think more and more about what David was saying. I began to take the food he offered me off his own plate when we were together. Maybe there *was* something to this brown rice. *Maybe.* It seemed crazy, though —extreme. I had to stay calm, or this whole thing would blow up and the entire family would become involved. Everybody would take sides. That was the worst thing that could happen.

Although I sometimes thought about what David was saying to me, for all practical purposes, I continued to ignore David's advice and to disregard my body's signals. I kept eating what I had always eaten. I did not want to examine myself.

Turning my thoughts back to the present, I see clearly that I must have had cancer for a very long time. I became aware of Frank watching me, still standing with his hands in his pockets as I had left him when I drifted off into my own thoughts, after telling him I intended to go to Amherst right away. How long had I been lost in my thoughts about David, The Bay, my wonderful children helping me?

Somehow, amidst all his protests, I convinced Frank that I needed to go to Amherst that day, so I could attend the macrobiotic seminar. I told him, "I have to go."

I don't know why I agreed to go to the seminar, months before. I guess it finally boiled down to the fact that I wanted to do what my children wanted me to do, and they were so persistent about it. I didn't know what I would find in Amherst, and I didn't really think about it.

Now that I knew I had cancer, going to Amherst to find out about macrobiotics was an alternative to surgery and chemotherapy, and one which I considered worth pursuing. I remember smiling wistfully at Frank and hoping that I was doing the right thing . . . .

---

[1] Macrobiotics is the art and science of achieving health and happiness by living in accordance with the ways of nature. Literally, "macro," means "large," or "great," and "bios," means "life." Together, they form the word "macrobiotics," or the opportunity to experience a great life filled with adventure, freedom, and creativity.

[2] Practitioner of medical diagnosis through clairvoyance. He died in 1944.

[3] The East West Foundation is a non-profit educational organization that teaches macrobiotic principles throughout the world.

2

Two roads diverged in a wood, and I—
I took the one less traveled by,
And that has made all the difference.
                                        —Robert Frost

THAT SAME AFTERNOON Melissa drove me from Vermont to Amherst, Massachusetts. Frank bundled me into the car. It's August, I thought to myself. Why is he putting a blanket over me? He tucked in the edges and told me to take it easy. How else could I take it, considering how awful I felt? I looked down at myself and tried to smile, but things were such a mess. I couldn't find the right button. I hung my head as Frank brushed my hair with his lips.

"Take care of Mother," Frank directed Melissa. "Be careful." He ran his hand along the door after he closed it. I placed my fingers on the edge of the open window. He covered my hand with his for a minute, looked at me carefully, then backed away from the car. "I'll be thinking about you," he said, holding the back of his hand to his forehead.

"Frank," I said, "we'll be fine. We'll see you tomorrow night." I didn't have the energy to wave.

We drove out of the driveway and down the road. I watched Frank getting smaller in the side mirror, standing by himself in front of the house—a compact, sturdy, gentle man. Was he hoping we wouldn't speed away from him too fast?

* * *

It was Tuesday, still the same day it had been this morning

before I went to the hospital, but, oh, how it seemed like another year! Already I was feeling old and worn out because I was supposed to die. I had to laugh at the thought of my dying. I've raised six children, moved them here and there all over Vermont, nursed hundreds of people, cooked, cleaned, worked, strived, hoped, been happy and sad and hopeful about living to be old. What the doctor was telling me today, though, is that I'm already old in my lifetime. Elderly, in fact. *What* was this about dying?

Again for the second time today I was speeding down the highway, considering my own destiny. I hadn't felt well at all during the past six months. I was losing weight fast, my skin color was terrible, and the mole on my arm—well, that was the clincher. I hadn't wanted to face up to that. I couldn't convince anyone I wasn't aware of what was happening, least of all myself. I knew the signs. I rubbed my arm where it was bandaged.

"Does it hurt?" Melissa asked me.

"What's that?" I said.

"I asked you if your arm was bothering you. We have those pills the doctor gave you if it starts to hurt."

"No, no, it's fine . . . ." I went back to my thoughts.

I would have been furious with anyone else if she had ignored the signs as I had. I couldn't stand it when people wouldn't do anything to help themselves; when they acted stupid. Yet I had become that kind of person. Why, I wondered to myself, did we feel we were exempt from our own best advice? Why do we have all the answers for everyone else and never for a moment listen to our own best philosophy?

"Deb says people get better all the time with this diet," Melissa broke the silence in the car.

"*I* believe it," I said. I sure hadn't seen people getting well from surgery and chemotherapy and radiation treatments. Children, teen-agers, healthy looking people with families, with people depending on them. I had seen them all go—. Yet the doctor was telling me I *must* (and this was his word),

I *must* (kept repeating it to myself) have this therapy. Or I would die. Or did he say I would die anyway?

I thought about my disease. "Malignant Melanoma." What did the words mean to me? Well, first of all, they implied that I would die. But what else? What about the words themselves? I thought about it, saying the words over and over to myself. "Malignant melanoma." "Mali*g*nant Melano*m*a." "*Malignant*"—the word sounded as if there were no bounds to the destruction of which it was capable. The word just oozed dark, spidery trouble. It sounded like a word that had been made up specially for Halloween, or to describe the sinister cliffs in a gothic novel where the hero is about to be viciously murdered. "Malignant" was a difficult word to ignore. The word "melanoma," when coupled with the word "malignant," rolls off the tongue with such ease, it seems to gain authority as the m's spill out of the mouth, compounding themselves with terrifying strength. What if, earlier this morning the nurse had squeezed my arm and told me I had a disease called, "Isle of the Pacific?" It wouldn't seem so bad, of course. Dying is frightening enough. But these terrifying names make a person feel even more alienated from herself. Oh well, a minor point really. The main thing is, I'm going to die of this disease, whatever it is called. "Dis-ease," as Edgar Cayce put it. Come to think of it, I did feel uncomfortable with myself.

"Does this bother you?" Melissa had just switched on the radio.

I told her "no."

I can't give up, though, and just let this malignant melanoma wrap its churlish fingers around me and take me away from my family. I looked over at Mel, driving. She looked the way I'd wanted to look when I was her age—pretty, dark-haired, doe-eyed; simple, graceful, and *calm*. Would she stay peaceful if I died?

When we drove to Alaska a few years back with our children and some friends, we were two cars and a truck. A young boy jumped out in front of our truck just over the Canadian border. Frank was driving, I was in the front seat, and our children were in the back except Deb, who was married by then and traveling in another car with her husband. I remember the boy walking out in front of the car—he must have been daydreaming, but all of a sudden there he was. Frank jammed on the brakes and swerved off the road into the embankment. The truck was badly damaged, but none of the passengers were hurt. The young boy, however, had been knocked down, as the back of the truck swung around. The boy turned out to be fine. Frank was badly shaken, and he announced, standing over the wreck that had been our truck, that we should forget about going to Alaska and that we should go home. I had told him that I thought we should keep going. We had come this far, and we were all excited about seeing Alaska. Eventually he was convinced, and we stayed in that town for three days while our truck was being fixed. After making sure the boy was all right, we continued our journey north and had a very memorable trip camping and exploring in Alaska. We are all very glad that we decided to keep going after the accident.

We had done a lot of terrific things. I thought back over the years to when the children were younger. We each went our own way, Jeffrey building his log cabin in the woods on our land; Deb coming home from college and telling Father, "It makes sense what they do in China—communism," and Frank getting madder than when he cut, split, and stacked three cords of basswood that wouldn't burn; Dexter playing his music; Judith and Melissa riding horses, bringing home stray animals and sleeping together with a flashlight between them; David taking off for Europe when he was seventeen with one hundred dollars in his pocket and no plan. Well, their parents weren't much better. I had to laugh. While our children were doing normal, childish things, so were we.

People in the suburbs often borrow sugar from their neighbors. Well, we did that too, out in the backwoods. But our neighborliness extended beyond the mere pleasantries. It's true, we stuck up for each other (we had to, winter in Vermont can be a life-or-death situation). For entertainment we stole each others' hens and cows, tractors, cars, trucks—anything we could get our hands on. It was all in fun, and there were many nights we were all running around, sliding over the frozen ground, trying to locate a missing animal or two. We had a running game going, which lasted twenty years. Mostly it was the Browns and the Bumps. I shook my head and laughed.

"What?" Mel asked.

"I was thinking about the Bumps," I said. She laughed. I hand't seen her laugh yet today.

I was grateful to Mr. Bumps, who was a very large, strong man, for carrying me down the hill by our first house in Vermont, down through the mud which was ankle-to-calf deep. Down, down in the middle of the night in mud-season to Frank who was waiting in the car at the bottom of the road. I've thanked him again and again in my thoughts as the years go by, for not saying anything about the fifty pounds I had gained, or the mud oozing up over the tops of his boots, as he carried me, hemorrhaging and about to deliver, down the impassable road. This was not the neighborliness you see on television when you talk over a fence or wave as you pick up your morning paper off the front walk. We wouldn't have made it that night without Mr. Bumps. And Melissa wouldn't be driving me south to Amherst today, for it was she who was delivered into this world that night seventeen years ago in a hospital in White River Junction.

I remember when we first moved to Vermont. There was something that impressed me immediately about the state. It was different from any other state I had visited. It wasn't just the incredibly green hills or the immaculate farmhouses; it wasn't how the sky seemed to hang protectively over the land or the fact that there were no billboards along the sides

of the roads. The land was untouched and yet there was a
civilized air about it. Vermont seemed very traditional to us
in the true sense of the word; life there appeared to be based
on the same common sense values that our ancestors might
have used, and when we moved there and became a part of it
and felt comfortable, we saw that it was so.

In the late 1950's, land was inexpensive on the outskirts of
Woodstock and when we saw two hundred and fifty acres of
the most beautiful land we'd ever seen offered for sale at a
price we could almost afford, we went to see it. I could see
in Frank's face that he was in love with it. We took out a
loan and it was ours for $20,000. We had five children then,
and not much else. Wait a minute, that's not exactly true.
We had a lot of strength and a lot of drive, and we were very
young.

Frank cleared a dirt road through the land and built a house
near it. We painted it red. While he was building, the seven
of us lived in a cabin, also on what was now our land, which
we called "the camp." The Bumps were our neighbors down
the road, and the Richardsons were our other neighbors.

We built many houses after that, slowly, during the twenty
years we lived outside of Woodstock, and sold them in order
to support the needs of our growing family. We grew our
food and built our own shelter. Our children walked to school,
breathing clean, clear air. We had everything we needed. I
have heard it said that the per capita income in Vermont is
the second lowest in the United States. If this is true, it is
undoubtedly because there isn't as much need for money
changing hands in this state as there is in the other states.
A man drags three dry logs onto your land in September and
leaves them there without being asked. In March you leave
ten gallons of maple syrup at the door to the same man's
house. There are people these days who call this bartering.
We never called it anything. It's just the way it was. I hope
it will always be this way in Vermont. I hope we will always
understand and respect these very special values and protect

them from any encroaching hardness which separates us from the needs of others. Nestled between Canada, Maine, New Hampshire, Massachusetts, and New York, Vermont seems like an island to me where things remain pretty much as they've always been, as if the state were surrounded by water.

Where else could our children have grown up as they did? Dexter tells me he had no idea what money was all about, never had to worry about it. I wonder if that view was too unreal, and therefore unfair to our children. He says how grateful he is for learning about the true value of things.

I remember helping Jeffrey drag the logs he had made to the site he had cleared by himself. No one had paid much attention. Jeffrey was quiet, and everyone else was busy with his own interest. I loved big challenges, especially those I could solve with my hands. Jeffrey and I had practiced for building the cabin by taking apart an old jeep the year before and putting it back together again.

The same year Jeffrey built his cabin, a darling girl with long reddish hair and a broad smile found her way into our kitchen and started talking to me. She was interested in everything and glanced around often. We talked about things people her age were interested in in those days—the Vietnam War, politics, religion, even reincarnation. There were a lot of young people staying at our house then. We were used to a house filled with our children's friends, but especially now there were always five or six or even more people staying with us. And they were young adults now, the same age as Deb and David and Jeffrey. Some were older. It was a difficult time to be eighteen to twenty-five years old we realized, as our home became a comfortable place for young people who felt like outsiders in their own homes. Aside from grappling with the usual problems of growing into adulthood and trying to answer questions like, "Who am I?", they were dealing with a difficult, fast moving time in history. I don't know exactly why these young people felt more comfortable with us, but they said they did. We accepted them.

I think this young girl who came to visit that day—her name was Julie—was amazed at the goings-on in our house. There were people everywhere, visiting for the week or the week-end or the day. She had mentioned whom she was looking for when she first came to the door, but after she saw the contents of the house I don't think she could remember why she had come in the first place. My maternal instincts told me it was Jeffrey, and my instincts turned out to be right.

Soon after, Julie and Jeffrey moved into the cabin he had built in the woods. They lived there for four years, during which time they got married. They cooked and heated with seven cords of wood a year and had no running water or electricity. They were very young to know what they wanted,

The log cabin Jeffrey built when he was 16.

but they are both very stable and clear-thinking. I never worried about them.

David went to Europe and made his way around the continent, finally coming home to be an integral part of the home life to which Julie was exposed during her first visit to our house that day. David brought a dimension into our lives for which we were totally unprepared and which was common at that time in many households throughout the country. Looking back now, it is difficult to remember how helpless Frank and I felt each and every day, as we saw David getting himself more and more deeply involved in a lifestyle that we felt was immoral and potentially dangerous, as well as being unfamiliar to us. David was experimenting with drugs on a daily basis. We knew that some of our children had taken drugs, as had many of their friends, but David's fascination with drugs ran deeper. They seemed to appeal to his extreme nature. The more he indulged, the more difficult it became to reach him with any kind of reason.

At the same time, our children were telling us that the war in Vietnam was wrong. They said we were fighting a war that didn't even really exist; that the American boys who were dying over there were dying for nothing. This enraged us.

Frank and I were broad-minded, liberal, thinking people. We were very disturbed by the things our children were telling us. They exposed us to ideas we would otherwise have overlooked. As we became less hostile to what they were saying, we began to open up to the extent that we could consider points of view that would otherwise have been out of our range. Driving along in the car, as Melissa drove me to Amherst, I had no idea that the difficulties we had had with our children in the sixties and early seventies, and the resulting awareness that came out of them, would help me to be supple enough in my attitudes during the coming months, that I might embrace something totally new, totally unconventional, in order to help myself in my own difficulties with cancer.

We were pulling over to the side of the road now, as Melissa wanted to stretch her legs. She must be getting sleepy. It was growing dark, and I hadn't been a very lively passenger, lost in my own thoughts. I had the feeling, though, that Mel hadn't wanted to talk anyway. Too tired to move, I asked her what it was like out, outside the car.

"Very hot," she said. "And humid." Her hair was hanging limply around her shoulders.

"Are you all right, dear?" I asked her.

"Yes," she said and started the car. "My foot had fallen asleep."

How many times had I sat with a baby asleep on my lap, looking at the wall, watching the seasons change out the window? It seemed I was still holding a sleeping·child to me, warming to its needs, holding its head just a little higher so we could smile at each other. Which of my babies used to laugh at me when I did that—was it Debbie . . . or Judith? Was it Dexter? I wrapped my arms across my chest and tucked my fingers behind my back. Perhaps *I* had become the tiny baby, waiting for its needs to be met.

"Remember when you hooked up the washing machine and dryer?" Melissa asked, twirling a strand of chestnut hair around a long, slender finger. I laughed in response as I remembered the audience of kids watching me as I pretended I knew exactly how to hook the things up. Actually I had absolutely no idea how to do it, but there was no one around who did, and there was a mountain of laundry to do—and after not having had a washing machine and dryer until that moment, I was darned if I was going to trudge off to the laundromat. I hooked it up all right, and no one was more amazed than I, but the dryer didn't last. One of the kids staying at the house decided to dry three bushels of mint in it, and it was never the same after that. (It seemed he be-came impatient when the mint didn't dry fast enough by simply hanging it upside down in bunches all over the house.)

"*Whatever* made you think of that?" I asked Melissa.

"I don't know. I was just thinking about all the things you can do—how you always do what you set your mind to."

"You're like that too, you know," I told her.

"Yeah, but not like . . . ."

"Yes, *just* like that. You don't make a big fuss; you just go and do it."

"I never hooked up a washing machine and dryer," she said.

"No, but you could . . . and you probably will someday."

"Mmmm," she murmured, and we were again lost in our own thoughts.

I couldn't believe this was all really happening to me, to us, to my little Melissa, to my dear, wonderful husband. Oh, Frank. What was he feeling? What was he wondering right now, alone in the house in Ferrisburg, a house that wasn't even ours. What was he thinking about our future, as he paced inside our temporary house? Would I live to see the next house? We had moved often during our life together. Would this be our last move together? The doctor this morning said that *Yes*, this would be our last time together, for Frank and me. I wanted to say *No*, because why—why was it so and could it really be as simple as that? He says I have cancer, and then a little while later, within the alloted six months, I lie down and say good-by to all my dear ones— family and friends alike. There was a terrible absurdity in this, and a deep, searing pain ripped through me like lightening. I wasn't sure where it came from, didn't know how much damage it could do, and most of all, I didn't know if it would be back. It wasn't a physical pain, it was an emotional one, and it hurt worse than any physical pain I could imagine.

Apparently I was supposed to sit around and wait to see if the doctor's prognosis came true. But I was riding in a car going to Amherst, Massachusetts, because of a loving family that nudged me to see if there might just possibly be something more we could do to face our problem. In a way, things had fallen together as if planned. I had registered for this

seminar months ago, and here it was, scheduled to begin
tomorrow, precisely when I needed it, for there was no time
to delay. Even if it didn't turn out to have anything to offer
me, I would know that by tomorrow night, and could start
thinking about an alternative. I guess there are psychiatrists
who would say I was in the "denial" stage of dealing with
my cancer. In a way, looking back, that assessment is profoundly true, because it wasn't until later, when I had fully
accepted the disease and recognized it as my own and of my
own making, that I could begin to rid myself of it.

We had spent our lives drifting in and out of things. I
can't remember "planning" anything the way most people do.
Like The Bay. One day we were living in Woodstock as
we'd been doing for twenty years, and then the next thing
we knew we had moved our family, our belongings, and many
of our friends north more than one hundred miles to the old
"L'Ecole Champlain." I can't think of a single practical reason
why we did it. The opportunity simply presented itself, and
I guess we were ready to move from Woodstock. The gen-
erosity of a member of our family made it possible for us to
purchase the exquisite piece of land, and we realized ex-
citedly that we had the opportunity to build the community
we had always dreamed of. Our oldest child Deb and her
husband Philip had always wanted to run a school. At The
Bay, they had a school for fourteen children, many of whom
were in the care of the state. Deb and Philip did fine work
there, and they were able to continue with it after we sold
the land. All of a sudden Frank and I were father and mother
to these children as well as to the other young people living
in the community at The Bay. We had a restaurant serving
natural foods, prepared primarily by Julie. The school, the
restaurant, the rural community were all dreams we had.
Suddenly we were living our fantasies. We never seemed
to think ahead and consider what we were doing; we came to
Woodstock in the late fifties and just began to live, taking
each day as it came. If we didn't know how to milk a cow, we

learned. If it took all day to clear our dirt road after a snow-storm, then so be it. Vermont weather can be harsh, but we learned to go with it, not to fight it. Things are usually easier this way. We may have stumbled over the rough terrain, but we nevertheless got over the hills and the valleys and reached our destination. What's more, we were very pleased to be there when we did.

People who are used to conducting their lives in an orderly way find our way of life difficult to understand, and even frightening. And yet, for all the things we've lost—money, land, material objects, I feel we have experienced fully what each day had to offer. Childlike in the sense that our judgment wasn't always sophisticated, we were also childlike in our

A friend helps with lunch at the Brown's Woodstock home in the 1960's—rows of white bread smeared with peanut butter and jelly!

enjoyment, as we seemed to find opportunities everywhere, and whatever disappointments we experienced, like children, we were able to shrug off as our attention was captured by something else.

When Debbie Quinn married our son David, she seemed to relax into our family, finding contentment with the way we lived. Our family seemed warm and open. It was she who looked at me so earnestly after David had left the room that day, months ago, when I had made the decision to go to Amherst. It was she who said, *"Please* go, Mother." Her eyes pleaded, "Please . . . ." It was that night that I told her, as my granddaughter Jessica curled up in my lap, that I would go. I have no idea why I agreed, except that they asked me to go. There was no reason to resist. And I was curious. What was the harm? It was a long way off anyway . . . .

I had no idea I would really *need* to go when I told Debbie, "Yes." Well, she and Judith would be meeting us in an hour or so . . . I looked at the clock in the dashboard.

"Not long now," Melissa said, acknowledging my glance at the clock. "Judith and Deb said they'd meet us at the motel."

Judith was driving up from New York. Had anyone told her or Deb that I had cancer? I realized I would have to tell them when we arrived.

I closed my eyes and tried to rest until we arrived in Amherst. I kept seeing our kitchen table as it had been in Woodstock, covered with white squares of bread—two or three loaves, with peanut butter and jelly being spread onto them. This was lunch at the Browns back when the hay was stacked neatly in our fields, back when the hills held us snugly with their rolling hug, back when I would look out the kitchen window to see our children running all over the countryside, and the upholstery on the chairs in the livingroom by the fireplace was worn down to the springs . . . .

3

If we leave nature alone, she recovers gently
from the disorder into which she has fallen.
It is our anxiety, our impatience, which spoils
all; and nearly all men die of their remedies,
not of their diseases.

—Molière

FINALLY, WE ARRIVED in Amherst and met Judith and
Deborah in the parking lot of the motel where we had
reservations. I told them the results of the biopsy that
morning, and I was surrounded by the suffering of the three
girls. I knew I had to do something to make it stop—but
what? I was so tired, I couldn't think of a way. It was decided
that Judith would be coming home to Vermont to help, so
she and Melissa drove to New York to get her things.
Deborah stayed and went with me to the conference.

* * *

At noon on August 23, 1978, I walked into the Buckley Music
Hall at Amherst College and said a silent prayer that, within
these four walls, I might find an answer. Deborah and I took
seats near the front of the hall and waited for the program to
begin.

I sat quietly in my seat, staring at my hands. They were
skinny and wrinkled, and greenish-gray. I wondered what they
had to do with me. Certainly they bore no resemblance to the
strong, smooth, capable hands I had always had. I had always
thought my hands were my best feature. Had I been mistaken
all these years? Was I only now seeing the way my hands

really look—or had they changed drastically? They didn't look exactly old, I thought, turning them over in my lap, they just looked odd. The shape was different, they were puffy.

"Mother?" It was Deborah. "Are you okay?"

"Sure, dear. Fine . . .," I replied, and went back to examining my hands. I just couldn't figure out when they had changed.

When I looked up, the bright lights overhead burned my eyes. I squinted and saw that the hall was full. The same questions filled me as they often did when I was at work at the hospital—where do all these sick people come from, why are there so many people with incurable diseases? It seemed that these days there were more desperately sick people than ever. And now, I was one of them.

Deborah looked at me and picked up my handbag, which had fallen to the floor.

"Don't worry!" I told her. I couldn't stand her sad face. "Just tell me what's going on," I said impatiently.

We settled back in our seats and the room grew quiet, as a young man took the stage . . . "Ladies and Gentlemen," he began, "before we start this afternoon's program, I would first like to welcome you to the Second Annual Conference of the East West Foundation on the topic of *Nutrition, Cancer, and Degenerative Illnesses.*" He was a light-haired man about forty, with a round, pleasant face. He continued, "I'd like to introduce some of our special guests here . . . ." He motioned off to his left, where about ten people sat on folding chairs. There were three women, two were wearing kimonos. He went on to introduce these people, whom he described collectively as "the panel." I don't remember everyone; however, Aveline Kushi, Michio Kushi's[1] wife, was there, and I remember wondering at how tiny she was. About thirty people sat on the stage of the music auditorium including a number of doctors and medical researchers.

Debbie said, "Look, there's Lima Ohsawa[2]!" and bent forward in her seat to have a better look.

The first speaker of the day was Dr. Robert Mendelsohn, Associate Professor of the Abraham Lincoln School of Medicine at the University of Illinois. He is well known for his syndicated column, "The People's Doctor," and as the author of the book, *Confessions of a Medical Heretic.*

I was interested to hear what the doctor had to say about this macrobiotic diet . . . .

His comments were in full support of the dietary program, and he used a rather unusual example to make his point. He told about a newspaper article which described the ex-POW's of the Vietnam War as being healthier than their contemporaries. Mendelsohn explained that while everyone else was eating the standard junkfood, as he called it, these prisoners were eating rice and vegetables, "the essence of the macrobiotic diet, really," he said. He turned this into a joke by suggesting that we might all be better off if we'd become prisoners of war. We all laughed politely, but I couldn't help

Michio Kushi addresses the East West Foundation Cancer Conference at Amherst College, August, 1978.

People in photo (from left to right):
Dr. Anthony Vincent, Marion Tompson, Nicholas Mattern, Marilyn Light, William Dufty, Michio Kushi, William Tara, Dr. Robert S. Mendelsohn, Dr. Chandras Thakkus, Dr. Edward Kass, Dr. Frank Sacks, Dr. Fred Ettner, Dr. Hajime Nishioka

sensing that most of us in that room already felt like prisoners, bound up, controlled, and set aside by our raging illnesses.

After Dr. Mendelsohn, Michio Kushi was introduced. He was slender and wore glasses. The first thing I noticed, as he began to speak, was his smile. It seemed to fill the room with a warm, playful quality. "Thank you for coming," he said, as if we were guests in his own home. He explained how, looking at us as if he saw each one of us individually, more and more people were experiencing the benefits of the macro-biotic diet... they were enjoying better health and better rela-tionships with their family and friends. He explained that there were as many as one million macrobiotic people through-out the world.

Without further delay, he outlined a common sense dietary plan which was impressive in its simplicity. He drew a dia-gram on the blackboard—a circle cut into uneven wedges, like a pie that was being divided for a family with different-sized appetites. He pointed to one section and suggested that we eat this relative proportion (50%–60% of the daily diet) of *whole* grains—he stressed the word, "whole," to discourage us from bread and cakes. These whole grains include brown rice, millet, barley, oats, wheat berries, etc. Then he pointed to a smaller wedge of the pie drawing and indicated that this was to be the proportion of fresh vegetables; 25% of the daily diet preferably locally grown, and cooked, rather than raw. He looked at the audience as if to ask if there were any questions. He was always smiling. I decided I liked him.

No one asked any questions, so he continued, pointing to the next-to-last wedge of the pie; this, he explained, com-prises 10% of the daily diet and consists of beans and sea vegetables. He assured us we would learn more about sea vegetables later. And last, he said we should have one or two small bowls of *miso*[3] soup every day. He said the word pre-cisely, as if he were pleased to be introducing a foreign dig-nitary to us. And then Mr. Kushi sat down to applause. No complicated formulas or combinations, no machinery, pills,

Michio Kushi/ © 1984 M. J. Maloney

or fancy manipulations. It was simple enough for anyone to understand. It seemed like a leap of faith, but I was ready to make the jump. What I had observed in nursing made me feel that the answer to why we suffer so much must be very simple. While we continue to make things complicated, isolating symptoms and parts of the body, the secret lies in synthesizing our understanding, rather than in fragmenting it. This really made sense to me in principle, this simple, non-dogmatic way of eating, because it represents fundamental change. It rang a bell somewhere inside me, because I knew that in order to get well, people need to embrace life. What better way to do that than to eat whole, clean, live food?

After Mr. Kushi, many people stood up and told their stories about what had happened to them. They told about serious, most often terminal, illnesses of all kinds. They were as bad as mine, some were worse. They had had cancer of all types, heart disease, reproductive problems, and so on. These were common, everyday problems that I was used to seeing day after day in the hospitals where I had worked for years. I searched my memory for patients I had known who had lived to sing the praises of the treatment they had undergone. While I am sure there were people who greatly benefited by the treatments they received in the hospital, my overwhelming impression was that of a lot of suffering which was met with little relief, especially in the case of cancer. The so-called "terminal" cases were most often not benefited by medical treatment.

However, these fifteen people at the conference were saying things like, "Back in 1967 . . . ," or "Four years ago . . . ." This is the first thing that struck me about their stories. They were saying how they *had had* these terrible illnesses—pan-creatic, uterine, breast, lung cancer, and they were speaking in the *past tense*. That was how *I* wanted to be speaking in a few years.

The one case that really interested me was that of Ms. Diane Silver. She told us about her past medical history, which read like a textbook, so common was it in its progression of illness. Eventually, her doctors had told her there was nothing more they could do for her. She turned to macrobiotics, at the urging of an acquaintance. She explained how, after going on this diet, her health problems began to fall away. Her tumors dissolved, she was no longer tired, she no longer suffered from chronic pneumonia, cystitis, and body aches and pains. And, of course, she had not died and was here to tell us, "Last year at my annual check-up my doctor said I'm healthier than I've been in years." She smiled at us and added, "My life has changed for the better." I had the feeling that this was a tremendous understatement.

This points up something that impressed me at this conference. What was being discussed and proposed here was spectacular in its effect on the quality of human life, and yet it was presented in a very restrained manner. At no time did I hear any shrill pronouncements about what this diet could do. Most of us in that room found ourselves in the very precarious position of being on the edge of death, and therefore susceptible to irrational promises for renewed health and life. It would have been easy to take advantage of such a group of people. Instead, however, I felt that I was respected as a human being, and what I heard was simple, common sense advice. In this fast, competitive world, I am grateful to these people at the conference, that they were not there to take advantage, that they did not hold out selfish hands to us, filled with empty promises, but rather they gave us something we could really use to help ourselves.

I really heard what Ms. Silver was saying. It wasn't just that she was more my own age, and I could relate to her better than the younger people who had spoken before her. I believed every word of her story, because it is not so uncommon, at least in its beginning. It is the ending that was drastically different, and that's what intrigued me. Her case history, up to the point when she started macrobiotics is, unfortunately, rather common, but most people just keep getting sicker and having more treatments. After the program was over, I wanted to speak to her. I wasn't able to stand in line for the food that was being served, so Debbie found me a place to sit on the grass outside, while she went to get me a plate of food. She brought Ms. Silver with her when she came back, and we spoke for a few minutes. Sitting there on the grass, I remember her last words to me. She said, "Try the diet . . . do it. You'll be very glad you did."

I thought about the other people I had heard speak at the conference. They had said how different they had felt after just starting the diet, that even if they had died anyway, as they had been told they would, they would have enjoyed their last days. Eating according to macrobiotic principles, they said, had given them a renewed sense of well-being. In time, this sense of life developed into the ability to get well—which they all did. I was so impressed and excited, overjoyed that I could actually do something for myself, bouyed up by the idea that I didn't have to rely on what I felt were the whimsical aspects of medicine (maybe this will work, maybe it won't; let's try it and see). I was very unclear about what could be gained from medical treatment. I had cared for many people with cancer, supported them through their ordeals with chemo-therapy, radiation, surgery, and the rest. Most of them seemed to get sicker, even those who made it through and left the hospital. A certain vitality was missing when they left. Many patients, however, had died, after having gone through the grueling and often heartbreaking treatment.

I had become a shadow of my former self—skinny, drawn, greenish in color. I dragged myself around, trying to get through the motions of life. I was already half dead. Medical treatment, I felt, would drag me down even further. I feared I would fall to a place so deep I wouldn't be able to get up.

Underlying all my feelings was a sense that I was able to get well. I realize I must have seemed like a person missing an arm, determined to use the arm anyway, but I desperately wanted to embrace life still and prayed for the strength with which to do it. I had procrastinated long enough.

The Brown Family, late 1960's. Back row, from left to right: Frank, David, Virginia, Deborah, Jeffrey. Front row: Judith, Dexter, and Melissa.

*　*　*

Judith, Melissa, and Debbie came home with me from Amherst. I remember they were busy making plans in the car, but I couldn't say what they talked about, specifically, as I slept most of the way, but their tone was very different from what it had been when I first told them I was sick, the day before. They were no longer sniffly and pale. They were chattering as always, laughing and making plans, shouting each other down with their ideas. I was so tired, I could have slept anywhere, and they weren't going to quiet down for me, anyway, which is just the way it has always been. There wasn't this huge word, CANCER, between us any more. We had all been infected with the spirit of helping ourselves, and we were a family again.

We rounded the bend and started down the road to our house. I thought of the beautiful land we had left behind on Lake Champlain. Our wonderful community at Kingsland Bay had eaten up all our savings, and we weren't making any money from the restaurant we had started there. We realized sadly we would have to sell the property. I remembered the faces of the land developers who came, anxious to buy the property for its commercial potential. They offered us a very high price for the choice land, one which would have solved our financial troubles, but we decided to sell the land to the state of Vermont, in order to protect and to preserve the natural beauty of the area. It was very sad for us to leave that place.

The state didn't want two of the buildings on the property, so Frank moved them to land nearby that we had kept. My daughter, Deb, and her husband Philip, continued to run the school in one of the buildings, while Frank and Melissa and I lived in the other house, nearby. It was to this house that the girls and I returned from Amherst that day.

Frank was on his bulldozer when we drove onto our property. It was raining, and through the mist I could barely make him out. He was moving boulders out of the way at the far end of the land, in order to extend the road. I thought it odd that he would be clearing in the rain. He was to tell me later that we were selling the bulldozer the next morning in order to meet our payment on the loan for Kingsland Bay.

The girls tumbled out of the car. Judith hadn't seen her father in some time, so she ran across the field, hopped up on the bulldozer (she had learned to drive on that bulldozer), and hugged Frank. I heard the sounds of their voices and saw their arms go around each other in pantomime made soft by the rain. I was exhausted and went into the house.

Inside, a lot had been done since Melissa and I had left the day before. The kitchen walls were plastered and papered with yellow flowers. I remembered my last efforts to help Frank with this house. I had been trying to shingle over where a window had been. I kept stopping to rest, sitting back on my heels, looking up at the hills. Finally, I had gotten up and gone into the house to sit down . . . .

I went upstairs and lay down on our bed. One thing was certain, I thought as I looked up at the ceiling which had a long, uneven crack in it—wherever we had lived (and we had lived in many houses), we had made it our home. I was just falling off to sleep when Frank came in and sat by me on the bed. He asked me how I was. I told him I was all right, but tired. I reached for his hand, wanting to tell him how different I felt, how things had changed since I'd gone to Amherst, how much stronger I felt—inside, how much I wanted to live and how confident I was that I *would* live. But, instead I fell asleep.

I awakened a few hours later to the sound of the door slamming downstairs and heard David's voice. The next moment he was bursting through the door to the bedroom. The world was always on fire for him. "Hey, Mom," he said and kissed me on the forehead. There is nothing half-hearted about David. Things are simple—you decide what you're going to do, and then you go and do it.

I told David that macrobiotics makes a lot of sense. He nodded his head enthusiastically and paced back and forth at the foot of the bed. "*Yes*," he said emphatically. I told him I wondered about the cooking. The idea of cooking anything, let alone foods I knew very little or nothing about, seemed like an insurmountable task. He told me not to worry, that he was telling Judith and Melissa how to cook for me properly. Judith had been a vegetarian for a couple of years, so she was at least somewhat tuned in to different, so-called "natural" foods, but Melissa—she had the eating habits of a normal teen-ager. I wondered about how the girls would do in the kitchen. During the coming months, I would see how incredibly well they did, preparing whole grains, vegetables, and beans, as they had never done before.

David told me Debbie was in the kitchen making dinner

and showing Judith and Melissa "the basics." Frank had come into the room while we were talking, and was sitting on the chair by the window, listening to us. He couldn't tell me what to do, couldn't give me support either way. I could see in his face that he was torn between advising me to take the surgery and the chemotherapy recommended by the doctor, and the seemingly crackpot approach his son was advocating. The medical approach had the advantage of being widely accepted and the disadvantage of not seeming to work very well in desperate cases such as my own. This alternative way that David proposed had the advantage of possibly working (who knows?) and the disadvantage of not having much scientific documentation. What could this poor man, torn between alternatives which seemed equally dangerous, possibly tell his wife?

He had stayed quiet. Our generation had never really questioned the status quo. Our children, however, had grown up in an age of questions—political, social, and moral. They had let their hair grow and their angry cries out, joining other young voices in calling attention to the injustices they saw in the Vietnam War. They opened their parents' eyes to the fierce need in these young people for the kind of peace and justice they felt, idealistically, to be the right of all living creatures.

David was looking at me where I lay, crumpled in my bed, with a challenge in his eyes. He would mock me if I refused to eat brown rice.

Debbie came in and placed a tray on the nightstand. She propped me up with two pillows and handed me the plate, which was filled to overflowing with the foods I had seen at Amherst. I recognized arame seaweed, brown rice, carrots, and black beans. I had lost thirty pounds during the last six months because I was unable to eat. I looked down at the plate of food which Debbie had so lovingly prepared, sliced scallions on the beans and toasted sesame seeds on the rice. It smelled good—something inside me stirred to eat, but I

hadn't eaten a plate of food in many months. Getting through
the food seemed a task like the days when we'd plow the
road to our house in Woodstock after forty inches of snow—
it took all day to clear a path through the mile-long road.
All I wanted to do was sleep.

"It looks delicious, dear," I said. "Aren't the rest of you
eating?" I asked them. "You're not going to stand there and
watch me, are you?"

"Of course not, Mother," Debbie said, "ours is waiting
downstairs. C'mon David, Father . . . ."

They left me alone. I reached over and put the plate back
on the nightstand and fell asleep sitting up as Debbie had
arranged me, smelling the sweet smell of food which had been
lovingly prepared for me, desiring for the first time in many
months, to eat. Sleep, however, won out, and whatever nourishment I got that day, I took in through my nose—and
through my heart.

The next day, Frank and I were alone in our bedroom,
talking. I told him, "I'm going to do it, Frank." He looked
at me, and I think he knew that it was true. He knew I would
do whatever I set my mind to. At least, I always had in the
past. But this was different, this was cancer . . . .

"What, exactly, is it that you're going to do, Jinny?"
Frank asked me.

"I'm going to eat a percentage of whole grains," I told
him, "barley, rice, millet and such, and vegetables, beans,
miso soup, and whatever else." I gave Frank the sheet with
the pie-shaped diagram on it that they had given me at the
Amherst conference. He looked it over and then back to me.
I knew he didn't think I looked any better than before I went
to Amherst, maybe worse. But I felt so optimistic!

"Do you think this will work?" he asked.

"Yes," I said, "I think so, Frank." He went downstairs,
where I knew he would talk to the girls about it . . . I lay
there trying to imagine what they were saying downstairs
and became frustrated with this. I decided to go downstairs

myself, and see . . . I stood outside the door to the kitchen and watched with eyes half-shut, my bathrobe pulled tightly around my shapeless body.

Deborah and Melissa were pouring over books and sheets spread all over the kitchen table. "Come on, Father, have a seat and look at some of this stuff," said Melissa. "Here, this is the one," she pointed to a recipe to Deborah. "I think we should make this."

"Okay, I'll wash the rice and the millet," Debbie said. "You get out the vegetables we'll need."

"Okay," Melissa answered. "When's David coming?"

"David's coming over?" Frank asked.

"Yeah, he's bringing over some pans," Debbie answered her father-in-law.

"Don't you need your pans at home, Honey?" he turned to Deborah. "I can go get what you need."

"That's okay; I'm used to these pans, and it would be better to start out knowing what I'm doing. I've been using these same pans for five years, and, under the circumstances, I don't want to make any mistakes."

"You'll be needing them at home, though, for your own cooking," Frank persisted.

"Father," Deborah turned to Frank, getting up from the the table to face him; she took his arms squarely in her hands. "Father, this is going to take awhile. I know we can do it." She groped for something else to say. "Mother is willing to try, and . . . so are we." She looked over at Judith and Melissa. "We'll be seeing a lot of each other for a while . . . maybe a long while. It all depends." I watched from the corner of the doorway. No one saw me standing there.

"Well," Frank dragged his fingers through his hair, "it's a heck of a way to get you kids to visit." He grabbed Deborah and tickled her. I went back upstairs. And as each bare foot touched a step, on my way up the stairs, I thought of a reason to be thankful for all that I had. As sick as I was, I was happy to still be at home, surrounded by my family, rather than set aside somewhere, in a hospital. In spite of the trauma that my illness was creating in our little world, I felt that things were still pretty much the same as always. My family was wonderful—they weren't afraid of me, now that I had cancer. They loved me as always, and they were going to *help* me.

Later, we ate the dinner that the girls had prepared.

"What's this?" I asked Judith. "It tastes good," I said, "but it's not exactly rice, is it?"

"It's rice with millet," Melissa answered, "pressure-cooked." She was eating a hamburger.

I remembered what they had said at the conference about chewing each mouthful many times in order to help digestion. "Don't forget to chew well, everybody," I said.

"Don't worry about me, Mother," Frank said. "I've been chewing for years." He, too, was eating a hamburger.

Melissa stuck her fork into the black, tangled mass in a white dish in the center of the table. "It's *hijiki*, Mel," Judith told her. Melissa fingered the dark, long strands of hijiki sea vegetable with her fork. "This looks really terrible," she said.

"It doesn't taste that great, either," I told her.

"Oh," Judith said, whisking a bunch of hair behind her shoulder, "you get used to it."

"I'm sure we'll grow to like it," I said. "*I'm* going to like it. I can just tell. There's something right about all of this." I waved my hand over the table.

Frank took a big mouthful of seaweed. "MMMM!" he said, before he had chewed, and then blanched after the vegetable had been in his mouth a moment. "It's a little . . . strong," he said, struggling with the words, "but good." He swallowed. "It reminds me of being at the ocean." He paused a moment, then lightened. "Let's pretend we're on vacation when we eat hijiki," he said.

When Frank went into the kitchen after dinner to help with the dishes, he couldn't get over how many dishes they had used to make dinner. "You sure use a lot of dishes cooking this way," he said, picking up two pans in each hand and carrying them to the sink. "It's quite a process." He shook his head slowly.

"The idea, Dad," Judith said, "is whole and clean—food that hasn't been, well . . . broken. Food that's well washed, cooked, cared for.

"It's like putting a baby on the table," Frank said.

* * *

Soon after we returned from Amherst, I decided to go to Boston to see Bill Tims at the East West Foundation. It had been recommended to me by the people I met at the Amherst conference that I see someone at the main office, in downtown Boston, who could tailor the macrobiotic diet to my needs.

One morning late in August Frank and I drove to Boston. It's interesting to remember the pressure we were under at that time, not just with my illness, but the fact that we had trouble getting together the money necessary to make the trip, is very revealing. There were problems in our lives at that time from all angles. I was to realize later that the money which we were able to borrow from our family in order to go to Boston was well spent.

We brought rice balls with us for me to eat while we were gone. Judith learned how to make them from David, over the phone. I heard about the process later from Frank, who was laughing so hard while he was telling me, that I could barely figure out what he was saying. It was something to do with the difference between a rice ball and a rice bomb. The ball is made by forming your hands correctly around the rice and making it into a round, flat patty. The bomb is made like a snowball—childish and ill-conceived. (I could see David scowling at the idea of these little weapons made out of rice.) When made properly, with a sliver of pickled plum in the center and covered with a layer of toasted nori seaweed, the food could sustain a person for a very long time. "It's the perfect food for traveling," David told Frank, who put Judith on for the details. It was she and Melissa who had made the black, stackable food which was nestled in the corner of my handbag.

We had walked away from our fiasco at Kingsland Bay with little more than we could fit in a suitcase. I thought this over as we drove south on Interstate 89, through Vermont. The air was clear and dew sparkled on the hood of our car. I chose, as we sped down the highway, to turn my thoughts to what we still had, which was a lot, which was everything in the world—our family, each other, a lot of love; and we were working on our health.

Frank switched on the radio, and we listened to the news report. How far away it all seemed! What did it have to do with the straight, tall trees covering the mountains on either side of us? What had it to do with the pavement stretching out in front of us like a welcome mat? I thought about the awful contents of the news report, no more unhappy than usual, but maybe even more disheartening for that very reason, and I realized that there was a lot of malignant activity in the world, and not just contained inside of people's bodies.

We drove straight into Boston, where we pulled up in front of an old, but well-maintained office building not far from the Arlington Street Church. We climbed the two very steep flights of stairs, following the arrows to the East West Foundation. I had to stop a couple of times along the way to rest. They don't baby you here, I thought to myself. I like that. They cater to health, not to sickness. They assume more healthy people than sick people will bound up these stairs. In the past, I never would have given these stairs a second thought. The obstacles in my life were becoming harder and harder to ignore. After all, now I could barely eat, barely walk; I was barely *alive*.

I stood back from myself for a moment and saw a middle-aged woman, gray-haired, skinny, yellowed, moving slowly up the stairs. A young man with a well-kept beard passed us on the stairs. He smiled. "What a wreck," he must have thought about me as he went by. He probably thinks I'm eighty years old.

Bill Tims talked to us in his small office at the East West Foundation. He was a slim, open-faced man with a ready smile. His hands came at me energetically to shake my hand, turn my head from side to side, to examine my fingernails. "I went to the conference in Amherst a couple of days ago," I told him.

"How did you enjoy that?" he asked in a Southern accent.

"It was wonderful." I noticed the music in my voice.

"Jinny came home from there feeling a lot better," Frank said. "She had a sense that she could help herself."

"Virginia, you're a registered nurse?" Bill asked me.

Bill Tims

"Yes," I told him, "for thirty-five years."

"And yet you decided against their treatment in your own case?"

"Yes," I answered him. "I've seen an awful lot of treatments that don't seem to work very well." I looked straight at Bill. I felt so sure of what I was saying. "I don't see cancer patients like myself getting much better . . . ." I thought about the people I've seen, lying in their beds, often dying —not anyone in particular, just a general impression. "That route is not for me," I said. "I've always professed alternatives, so here I am."

Bill told us, "Many people have good results with macrobiotics. The main thing seems to be whether or not the person, himself or herself, *wants* to get well."

I nodded vigorously, "Yes." I knew all too well what Bill meant. I had seen plenty of patients who weren't very sick just lose their desire to be alive, and they die.

"But let me emphasize that macrobiotics is not some type of medical treatment, but common sense advice about diet and life-style."

Bill smiled and continued, "The other thing which we have found to be essential," and he turned to Frank, "is that the family be fully involved and supportive." We all nodded in agreement.

"Now," he said, "what you need is a proper diet." He looked at me closely and pulled the lower lid away from my eye. "I guess you're fond of eggs?" he asked me.

"Well, yes," I replied. How did he know that?

Frank added, "It's her favorite food." He, too, looked amazed.

"You see," Bill continued, "the quality of the eggs enhances the development of your type of cancer. All meat, dairy food such as milk, cheese, and butter, sugar, and refined foods can lead to the development of cancer in general, but malignant melanoma, specifically, is brought on in part by the consumption of a large quantity of eggs." Then he asked,

"Are you eating macrobiotically now?"

"Yes," Frank and I responded together.

"Well, Jinny is, anyway. I think I'll probably do it too, pretty soon," Frank added.

"Tell me what you're eating," Bill asked me.

"Well," I thought, "Frank makes fresh oatmeal every morning—he grinds it up in our stone mill, just as he always has, ever since I can remember. So we still have that, only I don't put milk and butter on mine. Then, our daughters, Judith and Melissa, cook brown rice, azuki beans, kale, squash, carrots, things like that. Most of the vegetables come from our other children's gardens—well, from their cold cellars, this time of year," I told him.

"That sounds good," he said. "Just be careful to use whole rather than rolled oats."

"Our son, David, has been macrobiotic for a few years," Frank told Bill. "He's coaching the girls on what to make. In fact . . . here . . . ." Frank pulled a brown paper bag from my pocketbook. "These are rice balls. David told the girls how to make them so Jinny could have something to eat on our trip down here." He took one out of the bag. Some of the nori seaweed had frayed at the edges, but it was pretty much intact, otherwise.

"Gee," Bill said, "that looks good enough to eat!" We offered it to him, but he declined, saying he would be going home for lunch in a couple of hours.

During the next forty-five minutes, Bill explained the macrobiotic diet to us. It was the first time Frank had heard about it in such detail. It was the second time for me, but I picked up a lot of fine points I had missed at Amherst. I now understood the importance of eating sea vegetables. Bill explained to us that sea vegetables are very rich in minerals, particularly calcium and iron, two nutrients Frank and I had considered, hoping I was getting enough since I was no longer drinking milk or eating meat. Bill assured us we need not worry about my mineral intake, since the quality and amounts found in sea vegetables offered ample protection against experiencing deficiencies in these areas. This was incentive to get to like the strong-tasting food.

Bill pointed to a chart in his hand, a wheel like the one Mr. Kushi had drawn on the blackboard at the conference. "Here you see you should have 50%–60% whole grains," he looked up at me, "you know, brown rice, millet, barley, oats, corn, and so on—not bread. Do you know what I mean?" he asked.

"Yes," I said, "nothing that has been milled or processed in any way . . . ."

"Right, exactly," Bill said, and continued; "you need to have 25% locally grown vegetables. That shouldn't be any problem for you with access to your children's gardens. And then, 10% whole beans, especially chickpeas, lentils, and azukis, and sea vegetables, as we discussed before. Then, be sure to have at least one small bowl of miso soup every day. This is very important," he emphasized, "because the properties in the miso will help to make you well by detoxifying your system. Be sure to soak a piece of wakame seaweed and put it in the soup, as well. But," he smiled at us as he said this, "don't make the soup too salty. Miso is very tasty, but it will make you thirsty if you overdo it." He was making notes as he spoke.

"I'm writing these things down, and I'll give you this sheet" (the one he was pointing to earlier, with the food percentages on it). "The idea, by way of summation, is to eat whole, clean, unrefined foods which are found naturally in your surroundings. If you eat according to this principle, you will adapt beautifully to most anything that comes your way, including this cancer."

I asked Bill how long he thought it would take for me to get better. "Most people experience some change within several weeks," he said, and suggested that if everything were done properly, I might begin to feel substantially better in six months. Six months I thought to myself! I was getting to really like this alternative.

As we were leaving, Bill told us not to hesitate to call if any questions came up. "I think you're going to do very well," he said, as he walked us down the hall.

It was all so ordinary. Here was this nice, clean cut young man; intelligent, courteous, helpful, knowledgeable. He could have been doing anything. It was such a contrast to the doctor's office, where everything seemed so extreme, so apart from the outside world. Here, it was possible to think about everything in one thought. In the hospital it somehow was only possible to focus on a small part of life—a lung, a limb, or a surgical procedure.

What Bill Tims was describing to me in his friendly way was a life change—not a change in the little lumps under my arms, but a change in the way of looking at things, a way of life. It was far more fundamental, far more understandable to me. For the first time, someone was addressing the question, "How did it happen in the first place?"

"Well, no more eggs, Frank," I mused, as I picked my way down the two flights of stairs. I was leaning heavily on him.

"No, dear, no more eggs," he said. I wondered if that meant no more eggs for him, too. It's so hard to change, I thought, so very hard to question things you've done all your life. After all, we were nearly sixty years old. Hard to change, that is, unless you have a very good reason to want to.

We walked outside onto Boylston Street. Frank went into a local restaurant and bought a sandwich. We found a bench in the Public Garden near the pond and sat watching the swan-boats. He was eating a tuna fish sandwich and I was eating my rice balls. The sun felt good on the back of my neck. "Look at those two beautiful little boys," I said, as a mother passed us with her two young sons. The boys were leaning over the edge of the pond, trying to put their fingertips in the water.

"Watch it now," their mother said. "Don't go falling in

there." She caught each child by the elbow and held them in
one hand. With the other hand she broke off a piece of bread
which was sticking out of her purse, and gave it to the little
boys. "Now be careful," she said, "don't get too close to the
edge." They hopped to the edge of the water and started
tearing off bits of bread.

"Here, ducky, ducky; here, ducky, ducky . . . ." their voices
tinkled through the air. The bread broke the surface of the
water, and the ducks slid to the morsels and snatched them
up. They seemed to look up for just a second, as if to say
thank you.

Later that afternoon I went to see Bo-In Lee[4]. He lived on
a tree-lined street in Boston, in a nice old townhouse. Again,
I was confronted with stairs. I'd better get well, I thought to
myself, or I'm going to miss a lot. Many interesting people
seem to be at the top of a lot of stairs.

Blake Gould met me at the door to Bo-In Lee's apartment.
He told me he would be interpreting for Bo-In Lee.

The apartment was bare, except for a couple of mats and
a few plants. Bo-In Lee was at the other end of a large room
with a bay window. He came toward me and bowed. I bowed
in return. He was small and slight, dressed in a dark colored
kimono. It reminded me of when I was in Japan right after
the Second World War, as an army nurse. I stood still for a
moment, remembering the beautiful country homes and gardens I had seen in Japan. It was the beauty and the serenity
that I always remember from my military days in Japan,
rather than the widescale and horrifying destruction.

Bo-In Lee offered me a seat on the floor, on a mat, then
kneeled beside me and began to examine me from all angles.
He looked at my eyes and then at my palms. He told me I
was a healer. He also told me I would live in another country.
Just living at all would be okay with me, I thought. I was
glad he was talking to me as if I had a future. The nature of
that future wasn't all that important, although what he was
telling me did sound glamorous and worth living for.

Bo-In Lee went on to describe a series of corrective exercises which he felt would greatly benefit my condition if I did them daily, for about forty-five minutes. He described this to me through his interpreter. Blake was very patient —a good-looking young man who was obviously intelligent, considering his ability to understand Bo-In Lee and to make him comprehensible to me. Blake drew stick figures on a piece of paper for me, showing the different positions for my corrective exercises.

The main point, he said, was that my body was out of alignment. The right and left sides of my body were not balanced. He illustrated by pointing out how my left foot stuck way out when I lay down flat on the floor, while my right leg stayed straight. He smiled and said this imbalance would be corrected easily if I did the exercises every day. When the two sides of the body are not balanced, he said, it is very hard for the body to act together, in a harmonious way. This balancing act, he said, would make it easier for me to get well.

How did he know all this? How did they all know these things—Bill Tims, Michio, and the rest? How come we doctors and nurses didn't use these approaches?

Then Bo-In Lee showed me how to breathe. He placed me in a sitting position with my knees bent and my feet tucked under my bottom. He sat down next to me in the same way and took my hand in his. He placed my hand over his abdomen. I could feel the slow, steady extension of his body as he breathed. It was rhythmic and relaxed. He motioned for me to try. He placed his hand over my own abdomen while I breathed. It was difficult! Through Blake, he told me to practice this technique for proper breathing. Again, he placed his hand over mine and held it to his abdomen. "Proper breathing," Blake said, interpreting Bo-In Lee. "Do this every day, before meditating." He told me to visualize getting well, when I meditate.

I had trouble getting up off the floor when it was time to

go. Bo-In Lee helped me to my feet and made sure I was steady before he let go. He had been very patient. I felt he had given me more than I was aware of. Two hours had passed since I had arrived.

I descended the stairs from his apartment. He wished me well in Korean, understandable to me only in tone.

"Well," I said to Frank, who was waiting outside in the car, "it's been quite a day." I had the sheet of paper with the dietary recommendations from Bill Tims folded neatly in my pocketbook. I now added to it the sheet of stick figures Blake Gould had drawn. Strange, but I felt well protected, sitting there next to Frank, with these two thin sheets of paper tucked away in my purse . . . . It was rush hour, and Frank weaved his way expertly out of the city. We were on our way back to the green mountains of Vermont.

---

[1] Macrobiotic teacher.

[2] Macrobiotic teacher; wife of George Ohsawa, who first introduced macrobiotics in the West.

[3] Fermented soybean paste.

[4] Korean yoga instructor.

4

The best place to deal with cancer
is not in the operating room after the disease
has run its course, but in the kitchen before the
cancer appears.

—Michio Kushi

THE NEXT MORNING, I rolled myself out of bed onto the floor in order to begin the exercises given to me by Bo-In Lee. The sheet of paper with the stick figures on it was in my purse, by the bed. I took it out of my purse and smoothed it open, on the floor. I could barely lift my feet off the ground to do them, but I tried to do each exercise the prescribed number of times. It was frustrating, but I kept hearing Bo-In Lee telling me not to be concerned, that it was to be expected that they would be difficult at first, but that if I stuck with it they would become much easier for me to do, and I would be greatly helped by them.

When I finished the exercises, I heaved myself back into bed and lay there, feeling as though I'd just climbed the Matterhorn. Then I remembered that I'd forgotten to meditate. So, I closed my eyes just as I was, lying flat on my back, totally exhausted, and tried to visualize myself all better. I saw myself walking up the front path to David and Deborah's house. Jessie came running out of the house to meet me, and I picked her up and swung her around in my arms. I was smiling and had on a new flowered print dress that looked rather good on me. In my dream I weighed about thirty pounds more than I actually did at that moment.

A couple of days later, fully a week after I had had the

surgery on my arm, it was time to go back to the hospital
to have the stitches removed. Again, Melissa took me and
waited outside. I was reminded of the day the mole was
removed and I was told I had terminal cancer. It had only
been a week ago, yet I felt as if it had been months. Already
I had begun to change, if ever so little, and feel my intrinsic
ability to assert some influence over my future. I wasn't sure
what I could accomplish, if I could actually recover, but I
knew that I was going to try.

I felt out of sorts as the doctor continued his remarks, while
he removed the stitches from my arm. He told me I didn't
understand what would happen if I didn't have surgery right
away. He warned me there was no time to delay, no time to
think about it. He reminded me that no one *wants* to have
surgery. He said, "It's not really a matter of choice, in your
case." Not a matter of choice—what did he mean, that the
cancer had somehow infected my brain to the point where I no
longer had any judgment? Of course I had a choice. Stay
calm, I told myself. He's just telling me his opinion. I guess
I didn't answer him, because he sighed and tossed a piece of
gauze into the trash can. He didn't say anything more until I
was dressed and sitting in his office. Thank goodness Mel
came into his office with me . . . .

The doctor explained again that my type of cancer was
very serious, that I had a very short time to live. He suggested the surgery again, to remove my lymph nodes. I
squeezed my fingertips under my arms protectively. Suddenly,
my body felt lonely and exposed. "You waited so long before
coming to see me," he explained, "that we must act very
quickly . . . ."

He reminded me of my professional background and how
good medical judgment was a part of my every day. I could
tell he couldn't understand why I kept saying *no*. I felt sorry
for the doctor, trying to convince me. He was very kind, and
had, I am sure, my very best interest at heart; and I appreciated the medical sense of what he was saying. But I just

couldn't ignore the tiny, nagging voice inside me that said, "Don't do it." The most intelligent and well meaning doctor in the world couldn't have made me ignore that inner voice. The doctor looked at me so squarely, I wanted to go along with him. "Let's not delay," he said, getting up from his desk. I thanked him. Melissa took my arm and we left the room, and as we did so, I heard him tell his secretary to schedule me for surgery the following week. Melissa and I continued down the hall without stopping. I wanted to fold up the doctor's white coat, and lay it on a shelf . . . .

People have asked me why I was so sure about refusing medical treatment. Didn't I have doubts, they ask, or I really willing to die? I saw it differently. What the doctor was describing as my poor judgment, was really my self-knowledge that it was impossible for me to die—I would miss too much, and there were too many people depending on me; I wouldn't see my grandchildren grow up. I would heal, and my own body would do it. If I let them tamper with me, it wouldn't be my whole body any more, and I wouldn't have the ability to do what needed to be done. Unwittingly, they would take my natural ability away. Of this, I was sure.

Debbie Quinn was in our kitchen preparing food when Melissa and I got home. We had talked the night before, about what I was going to tell the doctor. "How'd it go?" she asked, and she seemed a little nervous. Did she think I would agree to what the doctor was proposing?

"I told him *no*, dear," I said. After all, I was a grown woman with six children. I did have some say, didn't I?

"I made soup, rice, and fresh kale from our garden. I thought you might be hungry when you got home," she said. Melissa turned up her nose and made a face. She started pulling bread and cheese from the refrigerator.

Debbie's cooking smelled good—*very* good, but I was so weary, all I wanted to do was lie down. I told her I'd eat later. Someday soon I knew I wouldn't feel so dragged down, and I would look forward to sitting up and eating with everyone. Right now, though, I took my old, tired body and laid it on our bed.

Later when I woke up, I told Melissa that I wanted to write a letter to the doctor at the hospital. She looked at me funny and then said, "Okay." She went to get some paper and a pen. "You write," I said. She settled into the chair by the window with the paper balanced on the phonebook on her knee.

Where to start?

I began by thanking him for his concern and for his excellent treatment of the mole on my arm. Mel was wondering what I would say next.

I told him I was going to follow the macrobiotic way of life, including its dietary plan. I explained that it included brown rice, beans, local vegetables, sea vegetables, and many other foods, with a special attention to proper cooking. I tried to picture the doctor's face as he read my letter.

"What's so funny?" Mel asked.

"Oh, I don't know," I said. "He's talking to me about cutting and chemicals—all that sophisticated jazz, and I'm telling him about soup. It reminds me of that science fiction movie where two worlds collide in outer space because they won't acknowledge the existence of the other; so, they simply bump into each other. Now, where were we?"

"You just told him what you *were* going to do," Melissa said.

"Right." I felt weak at the thought of how I was going to explain how macrobiotics "felt" right. Could I make my hunches sound believable? I told the doctor about the East West Foundation, located in Boston, where they were having good results advising people to eat a more nutritionally balanced diet. I did not want to sound like a nut; I just wanted to tell him what I was doing. I tried to keep my tone professional.

The letter wasn't very long. I realized the less said, the

better. I wanted to tell him about macrobiotics, but I didn't want my letter to sound as if it had been written by a crackpot. This was very hard to do, given the nature of the situation. "Do you have all of that?" I asked Melissa.

"Yup." She was reading back over it.

"What do you think?" I asked her.

"It's good . . . He won't believe it, but it says what you want." She brought the letter over to me so I could see it.

"Well, well, here it is, all in print." It was all bound up and sealed now. I had formally said what I was going to do about my cancer, and that was that. They needn't be bothered by me any more. I sank back into the bed and slid under the covers. "Mail that for me, will you?" I said to Melissa.

"Sure, Mom."

The world seemed lighter, somehow.

When I woke up, I heard the girls, Melissa and Judith, arguing. Then I heard Frank's voice say something firm, although I couldn't catch his words. Julie's voice was in the background. She seemed to be talking to someone else; maybe Jeffrey and Nathan were there, too. The screen door banged and the house was quiet. I wanted to know what had happened.

Later, when Judith came up with a tray of food that Deborah had prepared earlier, I asked her what they all had been arguing about earlier. Judith bit her lip. The scene was still raw in her mind. "What is it, Honey?" I asked her, lifting myself up on one elbow to look at her. Her blonde hair was covering her face as she set the tray down, and she was slow to straighten up.

"Father is going to sell the horses." She was touching the grains of rice that had fallen over the edge of my plate. "He said we have to." She was probably wondering whether or not she should be telling me this. It occurred to me that there was never any break in our lives, not even for my illness. Things just kept rolling along.

"All of them?" I asked her, referring to the horses.

"He said," she began, then waved her hand.

"You can tell me, dear. It isn't going to make me any sicker," I said. "I want to know what's going on around here."

"'We have to sell all of them—except maybe the pony. Melissa's sick over it. Maybe he'll let us keep Silver, too," she said.

"That means we're selling eight horses?" I counted them, subtracting the pony and Silver, because I knew Frank would never sell the girls' favorite horses. 'We had acquired these horses over the years; most of them had been given to us in return for work that Frank did. The horses had become as much a part of the family as our children. "Who's buying?" I asked her.

"Oh," Judith said, "different people." She seemed to spit this out. Our family was falling apart; she seemed to be saying. It was a highly emotional subject, selling the horses, and I know Frank wouldn't be doing it unless it was absolutely necessary. I felt like vomiting and wondered if I was just upset or if this was a new symptom of my cancer. I reached for Judy's hand.

"Come here, dear." She pushed against my shoulder, as I sat up in bed. "It's not that bad," I told her. "Things are going to be just fine. We still have each other." She nodded and put her arms around my head. "We're still a family, dear, no matter *where* we are."

"Mom," she looked down at me with her childish blue eyes, "are you going to eat dinner?"

"Of course I am," I said, and set right to it. Judith watched me, and I was glad to eat for her. She needed me to eat.

When she left, she told me that Melissa was very upset about the horses—that she had gone out of the house, banging the door behind her. Did I think she would stay out all night?

Who knows? She's seventeen. Her mother is dying of cancer, and her father is selling her horses, that she raised

like babies for nine years. It was a warm night; maybe she
would sleep in the barn and come home when she was ready.
How can you predict what a person will do under these circumstances? I told Judith not to worry, that Daddy wouldn't
sell Silver or the pony.

"How do *you* know!" she shot back at me.

"I know your daddy, dear," I said. "Now let me sleep."

In the morning, Melissa came up with a bowl of oatmeal.
The steam was rising out of her hands like an offering. I
hadn't felt fully awake until that moment; until I smelled the
warm cereal and heard her voice. Where had Frank been last
night? Had he slept next to me in this bed? I looked at the
pillow next to me. It was hard to tell. I hadn't heard a thing
since early last night, when Judith had told me about the
horses. Surely Frank had slept last night. Why didn't I remember? Where's your father?" I asked Melissa.

"Downstairs," she replied, and I could tell by the way she
said it that everything had been patched up. Probably, they
had made the cereal together this morning, which was one of
their usual ways of making up.

"How're you doing?" I rubbed her head.

"I guess you know about the horses," she replied. "That
we have to sell them."

"Yes, dear, I know about that."

"Did Daddy talk to you about it last night?"
she asked.

There was my answer. Frank *did* sleep in our bed last
night, right next to me. What was happening to me? Why
couldn't I get a grip on things any more? I told her, "No, he
didn't. I guess he figured you'd worked it out." I reminded
her, "Daddy wouldn't be selling the horses if he didn't have
to, Mel."

"I know," she looked down and twisted the edge of her
T-shirt. I knew she forgave him, but I also knew the pain of
separation would cut very deep.

"Love you," I said.

"I know," she kind of laughed, and left for school.

Later that morning, I turned over in bed and watched the tree outside our bedroom window, swaying against a fall breeze that was blowing in. I thought about our daughter, Deborah—Debbie Bouchard, we call her, now that there are two Debbies in the family. I hadn't seen her in weeks, and she was the only one I hadn't spoken to since the news of the biopsy report. I thought back to the argument we had had when she told me she was going to separate from her husband. How could she do that; he was family! I thought back over the years. In many ways we were like sisters. I missed not seeing her, but part of me knew why she was staying away. She probably didn't want to upset me any more than I already was. She was my firstborn, and we were so close. During all those years in Woodstock, sometimes it had been as if we had raised the rest of the children together . . . . It seemed that everything was happening at once, that our family was falling apart. We had lost all our money, Debbie and Philip were separating, and I was sick and evidently going to die.

The oatmeal was cold, sitting on the nightstand where Melissa had left it hours ago. I felt a little hungry—this was a newly remembered feeling for me. I picked up the bowl and began to eat. I liked the spongy quality of the cold mush. I would have given anything for a cup of coffee with it, but I made myself forget about that. I was going to follow this diet perfectly, and if it meant I wasn't going to drink coffee, well then so be it.

I looked back out the window. The tree was still swaying. An unseasonable day. It was still August, after all, and the air was blowing around as if there were colored leaves to lift off the trees.

Debbie Bouchard called me that night just to say, "Hi," she said. She asked how I was feeling and reminded me that

her daughter Tasha, would be starting first grade. I asked
her about Philip.

"He's fine," she said. "We're all fine, Mother," but she
evaded my question. It was as if we hardly knew each other.
I guess we were both trying hard not to hurt each other. I
noticed that my free hand was reaching out toward the wall
as I spoke to her.

"Tell Tasha not to be such a stranger around here," I said.
"Tell her to poke her cute face in here, so I can get a good
look at a first grader."

"Sure, Mother," she said. There was nothing more to say,
so we hung up.

Our children were all very busy during those days when I
first went on the diet. Julie and Jeffrey were living next door
raising their seven-month-old baby; David and Deborah and
Jessie lived about an hour's drive away; Dexter and Mary
were working hard on the recording studio they had just

Dexter and Mary Brown with their son Ki, in front of
their Vermont home.

started, and delighting in their newborn baby, Ki. And my wonderful girls, Melissa and Judith stayed with me day in and day out. They cooked and took care of me, giving up a large piece of their own lives, to help save mine.

Frank spent his time dealing with the last details of selling the Kingsland Bay property and doing the work needed on the house we were living in, so that we could sell it to meet our payments on the loan we had taken out for the land. He didn't say much during those days. He worked very long hours, and his spare moments were spent walking alone in the woods. Had I not been so desperately ill myself, I'm sure I would have worried a lot about Frank. He looked very tired and drawn. I think we all underestimated what he was going through, and focused on me. However, he was worrying more than anyone about me, about our financial ruin, and about our future.

A couple of days after I'd had the stitches removed from my arm, I received a letter from the doctor at the hospital, reiterating everything he had told me about my cancer and asking me to reconsider my decision about refusing surgery. He also asked me to come to the hospital to talk with the members of the tumor board. I realized that if I were a non-medical person and knew little about the profession, I might have been influenced by all of this. After all, the doctor's intentions seemed to be only the best. I believed, and still do believe, that he was acting in what he considered to be my best interest.

Later, Julie came by and I showed her the letter. She let out one of her great big generous laughs. "Kindness can sometimes do the greatest harm, huh, Mother!" She folded the letter and put it on the dresser. Judith came in from the store and told us she'd just seen her sister, Deb, there.

"How's she doing?" I asked her.

"She looks good," Judith answered. "She was buying eggs, though." She thought a moment, straightening the rug on the floor with her toe. "Can you believe she was buying *eggs?*" she asked.

"Why?" I sat up. "Because Bill Tims said my condition was caused largely by eating eggs?

"Well, yes, I mean . . . well, in view of *everything*," she stumbled. "Don't people listen? Or do they have to wait until their backs are up against the wall?" Her face was flushed.

"You mean like me, dear?" I asked her quietly.

"No . . . yes, well, you know what I mean, Mother. It's all so *confusing*, I mean *frustrating*, that's what I *really* mean. You know, it's one thing for Deb to eat the eggs, but she gives them to Tasha . . . she's making the choice for *her*." Judith looked at me earnestly.

"People don't change very easily, you know," I said. "We fed our kids plenty of eggs and everything else when you were little. We thought we were feeding you the best food we could. It turns out it wasn't so good. So what can we do now? We did the best we could. Besides, "I added, "maybe Tasha doesn't like eggs."

"Oh, Mother!" Judith was exasperated.

Julie let out another great laugh, which cleared the air.

"I love you, Mother," Julie said. I remember her saying this, because while she is lavish in her expression, Julie reserves her true feelings and reveals them only when she really means it.

A few mornings later there was a call from the doctor at the hospital. Melissa brought the phone in to me, and I spoke to him from bed. He wanted to know why I hadn't come to the hospital for the operation he had recommended, to remove my lymph nodes. I don't know if I was imagining it, but it sounded like he was talking to a teen-ager who had forgotten to take out the garbage.

I told him I thought I had made it clear that I wasn't

going to have surgery. He told me he knew how I felt and that it must be a very confusing time for me. He reminded me that I was a medical professional, and that surely I must know what this decision would mean.

I appreciated his concern. "However," I said, "the letter I sent you—did you get it? The letter explains what I am doing." And, even though I knew he wouldn't put much stock in it, I added, "I'm feeling much better since I've been eating this way."

There was a pause, and then the doctor asked if he could speak to Frank. I told him Frank was about fifty miles north of here, working. Actually, Frank had just walked into the room. I was so tired of all this. I thanked him again and hung up the phone. "Gracious!" I said out loud.

"What did he want, Jinny?" Frank asked.

"More of the same," I told him, and turned on my side to face him. "Why don't they just leave you alone?" I put my wrist over my eyes. "If you want to die, why don't they just *let* you?"

"Is that what you want to do, Jinny, die?"

"Of course not, silly, you all would never get along without me." He came over and held me. "Don't worry about *me*, Frank. You can worry all you want about the money we lost and about how we're going to pay everything back. But you're not going to worry about me, because I'm going to be fine. I mean it." He was looking down at my hand, which he was holding in his. It was scrawny looking and had an eerie green tinge. I snatched it away, as it seemed to go against what I was saying. I looked at him, "I'm going to be up, helping you real soon, you know."

* * *

The turning point came one beautiful fallish morning, two weeks after I learned I had terminal cancer and two weeks after I began the macrobiotic way of eating. I took a walk.

Frank got up at 5 : 30 as always and went downstairs to fix breakfast. An hour later, the sun was streaming in through our bedroom window, so I threw the covers back and got out of bed. I stood up and looked down at myself as if to see if everything was still there. I remember gathering up one side of my nightgown and twirling around in front of the window. The sun felt so good! I knew it was going to be a beautiful day.

When I was a little girl, I would hop out of bed each morning with great anticipation. My mother always said to me at the beginning of each day, "Tonight, before you go to bed, I want you to tell me something you saw today that was beautiful, something you smelled that was wonderful . . . ." I had the same eager feeling for the day to begin, as I wriggled into my clothes and hurried down the stairs. I could smell oatmeal in the air as I raced through the front door. "I'm going out for a walk," I tossed casually behind me, and I was outside.

When you take a walk for the first time after having been confined to the house for so long, and after having been so sick you couldn't tie your sneakers so you don't bother putting them on, when you're finally outside *moving around*, feeling the sun on your head and the reassuring touch of the earth below your feet—it's indescribable. I had a feeling of joy, of new wonder, of energy and rejuvenation, of complete faith. It was like spending a lifetime reading about Paris, and then finally going there. The journey from our bedroom, down the stairs, out the door, and down to the garden had been a long trip indeed.

From this point on, there was never any question in my mind that I would have died had I not changed my way of eating. The idea of change is very difficult for most people to grasp, yet we do it all the time, every minute of our lives. We change as a result of what we take in—experiences, sounds, ideas, people, air, and food! It is so simple to see when you live in the country. During my first walk that day,

I picked a bunch of dry weeds, beautiful muted flowers. As I
bent to pick them, I could smell fall in the air. Cooler winds
and clearer skies would soon be pushing through the hot,
humid air, and with a burst of color, autumn would settle in.
And when winter blew across these same fields, I knew that
I would be there to see it. I began to walk every day, working up to two miles a day.

* * *

In late September, I went to Boston to see Michio Kushi.
Vaguely, I remember when David and Deb had taken Jessie
to see him, and then again when Judith had gone to see him
with a friend of hers. At the time, I just thought this was
something the kids were all doing. I had no way of knowing
that I, too, would travel along the same path, in fact following
their lead. It was at this time that I remembered something
Michio had said to Judith, when he saw her back in 1976,
when she was there with her friend. When he was finished
talking with her friend, Michio turned to Judith and said,
"I want to see your mother." The way he said it made her
come home and tell me right away. His implication was that
I was very sick. I dismissed it as some kind of a silly notion.
In fact, however, I now realize that, through the practice of
oriental diagnosis, Mr. Kushi was able to see my condition
clearly reflected in the face of my daughter. This was two
years before I was medically diagnosed as having malignant
melanoma, stage IV, two years before the doctor described
my terminal illness to me and explained that it must have
been growing inside of me for a minimum of two years.

Debbie Quinn, Jessica, and I drove to Boston and stayed
in a hotel around the corner from the macrobiotic restaurant,
The Seventh Inn. It was 1978, and this was the only restaurant
of its kind in the area. I was still much too weak and sick to
enjoy Boston. I had grown up in Winchester, just north of
Boston, and had received my nurse's training in Boston, so

I was familiar with the city and had always loved it. On this trip, however, I didn't notice much of anything. Although I was much better since having changed my diet a few weeks ago, and certainly better than I was the last trip to Boston with Frank, when we saw Bill Tims, I was still so sick that the improvements could really only, at this stage, have been appreciated by my family and me. The city was a big blur to me that day. I didn't see the swanboats as we drove by, didn't watch the people, didn't even see the clouds reflected in the new, just recently completed John Hancock Building, that Debbie pointed out to me.

We arrived at Mr. Kushi's house in Brookline, a couple of miles west of Boston, and waited to meet with him. My impressions of the surroundings were very vague, simply that we waited quite a long time in the large front hall of his home. There was a big staircase at one end of the hall and many

David and Deborah Brown with their daughter Jessica, in front of their Vermont home:

people were coming and going, although it was very quiet.

I don't have any idea what I expected to find there. Having spent the past thirty-five years as a hospital nurse, even I, through the haze of my sickness, knew this was a basic, intrinsically different way of approaching illness. I was sitting on a damask upholstered setee, with my feet resting effortlessly on an oriental rug. I felt tired from the trip but comfortable, confident, and relaxed. The most remarkable thing was that I was going to see someone who, seemingly could provide insight into the reasons for my cancer—and still I had my clothes on! I was used to seeing patients waiting to see the doctor, shivering in their gowns which were slit up the back. In contrast to feeling like a patient or a victim of illness, I felt like an invited guest here at the Kushi's. It seemed we might break for tea at any moment. Lost in my tiredness and my dullness, I wouldn't have been a very lively guest, however.

When Mr. Kushi was ready, my legs were weak and Debbie looped her arm through mine to help me along. We were shown to the far end of the livingroom, which was lined with books. At the far corner, in an alcove with bay windows, Mr. Kushi stood up and shook my hand, then Debbie's. He smiled at Jessie and we sat down. He looked at me very carefully across a small, round table, smiling gently as he did, uttering an occasional "Mmmm . . . ." Abruptly, he relaxed back in his chair and folded his hands. "Cancer." He said the word with a combination of understanding and respect.

I nodded.

He leaned forward and said in a way in which I will never forget, "*You* made it, and only *you* can change it."

His words sank into me very deeply. Somewhere inside they bore into something that is essential to me—someplace I sensed was always there but had never felt before. Here was someone I had known for only five minutes who had touched something basic to me. At that moment I knew that I would follow macrobiotics, that I would get better, and that finally,

I would be well.

Mr. Kushi explained the diet to me, stressing that I should eat certain foods and avoid others. There was someone writing it all down. He told us to come back and see him in six months. This was very encouraging because, according to the doctor, I wasn't supposed to be *alive* in six months. When we left, we took the notes with us, but more importantly, we took with us a sense that it would work.

"What did he say, Mother?" Melissa asked when we returned home from Boston. She was the brave one, so everyone thought, but I knew better. Melissa befriended those who really needed a friend. She did the jobs that really needed to be done. She never spared herself, never gave in to feelings of fear or weariness. It was hard, sometimes, to remember that she was only seventeen. She had grown used to my slow responses during the last few months, so she waited patiently to hear what Michio had said.

"He said, *I* did it and only *I* can change it." I said the phrase out loud for the first time. It was to go around and around in my head; it was to be repeated time and again to family and friends during the coming months. I patted her arm and told her everything was going to be fine. Frank seemed to confirm this by coming in the kitchen at that moment. "You're mother's right," he said; "this diet seems to be working for her." Melissa told me later that Frank had told her not to make any more red meat for him—he wasn't going to eat it.

I went upstairs to bed. I was exhausted from the trip, and our bedroom looked fuzzy as I lay there watching the flowered wallpaper. I drifted off, as the wallpaper came to life. The bug on the wing flew to the flower, and the vines closed in on the trees . . . .

5

Healing is a matter of time,
but it is sometimes also a matter of opportunity.
—Hippocrates

A FEW DAYS AFTER my meeting with Mr. Kushi I visited the Association for Research and Enlightenment (ARE*) in Virginia Beach, Virginia. I had begun to look inward, considering my own needs, and what I saw was a strong desire simply to rest. As a working mother with six children, I had always considered the needs of others. Perhaps I knew that in order to survive, I had to begin to cater to myself a little. It was a difficult time for me to make a decision to go away, not just because my health was jeopardized, but because it seemed like a very frivolous expense for our family. We simply didn't have the $360 necessary to pay for my trip, and we had to borrow so I could attend the spa week. I am grateful that I was able to go, because during my stay at Virginia Beach I was able to relax and reflect on my situation. Like any good vacation, it provided the opportunity for me to gather my energy and regroup my thoughts.

Since the beginning of my fascination with Edgar Cayce, I had been interested in this research institute which had been set up in Virginia Beach as a kind of library for the Cayce readings and as a meeting place for people who want to find out more about Cayce's work. In *There Is A River*, Thomas Sugrue talks about how they chose the proper site for the institute, using guidelines set forward during the readings that Mr. Cayce had made.

It's amazing to me, looking back, that I had as much

enthusiasm as I did for going to the ARE, —considering how ill I felt, how I was barely able to perform the daily functions of life, how my interest in life, including my beloved family, was dwindling. But it had been a few weeks since I had been on the macrobiotic diet, and the changes were truly astonishing. There was a little spark inside of me that was beginning to glow. I felt the tiniest bit like myself again. I was not aware of this really, at the time, although I am sure Frank was, because he has since told me how relieved he felt during those first few weeks to see me walking, eating, talking, and even sometimes laughing. Although he was worried and unsure about my going off to Virginia Beach for a week, he was struck by my enthusiasm for going, my spirit for doing *anything*. I hadn't shown any vigor about anything in quite some time, since before the breakup of the Kingsland Bay community. He was nervous and also delighted to see me go.

I called Bill Tims at the East West Foundation in Boston and explained to him that I wanted to go to this spa week at the ARE. I explained that we would be having saunas, massages, and colonics and that we would be taking classes on subjects relating to the Edgar Cayce readings. I had also found out that the foods they serve there are very wholesome and that I would have no problem getting brown rice and vegetables if I went. I told him I believed in Mr. Cayce's work. Bill recognized readily the spiritual support this trip would provide for me. Macrobiotics stresses the importance of eating the right foods for your condition, but it also relies heavily, on the thoughts that are going on in a person's head and the feelings that are lodged in her heart. It is the whole person that is being viewed with macrobiotics, not just a piece of her. He encouraged me to go but advised me to adhere strictly to my macrobiotic diet. I told him I would. I wonder if, had I not gotten cancer, I would have ever gone to Virginia Beach.

For years I had been fascinated by the accounts of help Mr. Cayce gave to thousands of people who were suffering from serious illnesses. I never dreamed, as I read these accounts, that I, too, would one day be just such a desperate case. It had been previously just a hobby for me, learning about the wonderous way in which Mr. Cayce "went to sleep" and revealed life-saving treatments to those who asked him to do so. When Mr. Cayce went to sleep, he exchanged their desperation for a simple, accessible way of recovery. This is what macrobiotics was doing for me. The more I thought about macrobiotics, the more I realized it was all common sense.

Once again my family responded to my time of need and my desire to call upon something to help me get well. Judith got into the car and drove me to Virginia Beach, staying with me throughout my week there. She didn't say anything about what she was doing for me—none of them ever did—; they just did it. It wasn't a matter of their paying me back for giving myself to them when they were little and needed me; they were just helping me because it was needed, because they hoped as I did, and because they loved me and had confidence in me.

It was dark when we arrived at the motel where we were staying, across from the ARE. I met my roommate briefly, then fell into bed. I was very tired, but was unable to fall asleep. Thoughts of my grandchildren tumbled through my mind: little Ki in his mother's arms; Jessie and Jeremy playing out by the back door to our house discussing a pile of dirt they were making; how big Tasha was getting, her dark eyes turning adult-like; Nathan now just one year old. I wanted to know what they would be like as they grew—going to school, having dates, making lives for themselves. I wanted to see which ones would bite their fingernails and which ones would insist on having dogs. Maybe one of the boys would want to be a carpenter like Frank or his own daddy. Maybe one of the girls would want to be a nurse. Maybe . . . maybe . . . who knows . . . . And I wouldn't know unless I were there to see it. Oh, how I *wanted* to see it all!

I awakened the next morning and went to the window to look out. It had been dark the night before when we arrived, and I didn't really know where we were. When I looked out, I was amazed by what I saw. We were right on an absolutely beautiful beach.

"Pretty, isn't it?" My roommate turned over in her bed and watched my face as I lifted the curtain. "I got here yesterday and took a walk along the beach," she said. I put the curtain down and went over to her bed. I told her I was sorry we didn't get to talk much last night. It had been very late.

"You looked tired," she said, and asked me if I was feeling better.

"Much," I said, and looked down at her in the bed. She wasn't much more than forty, with light brown hair and a small, gentle face. I wanted to know more about her but wasn't sure how to ask. Not everyone who comes here has a health problem, but somehow I thought she might be sick —there was something in those eyes that told me she knew about suffering.

"I have Addison's," she said. "What about you?"

I was relieved at the way she had broached the subject and replied, "Cancer—melanoma, fourth stage." She looked me over, examining my face. "It's in the organs," I told her. She looked alarmed, and I patted her arm lying on top of the neatly folded sheet. "Don't worry," I said. "It's going to be fine. Now tell me about *you*."

"Oh," she lifted herself up on one arm and looked in the direction of the window. "I'm here because I want to get off prednisone. I've been taking it for fifteen years. My family is against my going off the medicine." She looked tiny in the bed, yet I could sense a deep strength in her, which drew me to her. I sat down on the edge of the bed, and we talked until Judith knocked on our door (she was staying in another room in the motel), telling us we'd better hurry if we wanted breakfast.

That morning, because I was late, I skipped my routine of

exercises and meditation, but for the remainder of the week
I was up early every morning, sometimes before the sun. I
did the exercises suggested by Bo-In Lee and then meditated
for about half an hour. Usually I recited the 23rd Psalm and
the Lord's Prayer to myself when I meditated. Then I walked
on the beautiful beach, sometimes watching the sun come up.
It was on that beach that I am sure I resolved a lot of things
—walking up and down, breathing that good air, the surf
pounding away, the earth squishing through my toes. I felt
connected to all that was around me. I didn't feel exactly
vital yet, but I sensed a bond between myself and all that surrounded me was too strong to be snuffed out. Anyone who
said I wasn't going to make it was just plain crazy.

After my morning rituals I had breakfast. Fortunately, I
was able to get brown rice there, and I had brought miso
with me to make my soup. After breakfast I went to class.
Then I had either a massage or a sauna. Also, on three occa-
sions, I had a very light colonic. This was not recommended
by the East West Foundation, but the kind people at the
ARE made sure that the solution was very mild. I don't know
if these treatments were helpful in the early stages of my
recovery, but I do know that this personal and tender individual care was very important to me.

The afternoons were our own, to do with as we chose. One
afternoon I wandered around the library which houses the
archives of the thousands of readings Mr. Cayce had made.
Other afternoons I spent with my roommate, having talks
which, to this day, I look back on and refer to in my memory.
We said things together during those times that have enriched
my life immeasureably.

Most often, however, I spent my free time walking on that
beautiful beach. I remember one afternoon in particular. It
was a bright, crisp day. As I looked out over the water, the
air was so clear, the water sparkled so, that I could feel my
eyes watering as they took it all in. I was wading in the water
up to my knees, when I turned around to see a young woman

walking a small distance away from me. Her head was down, covered with a brightly colored scarf. She was carrying a folding chair and her shoes in one hand, a newspaper in the other. She seemed to see only the tips of her toes as she walked brusquely down the beach. She seemed more than alone, she seemed lonely. As she passed, I wished something good for her—that she meet an old friend later, or that she receive a phone call or letter when she returned home that day. In the perfectly quiet afternoon, I wished silently that her life be happy and fulfilling for her. I could feel my heart going out toward this woman, bent over her chair, walking determinedly down the beach and out of sight. Could I have called out "Hello!" or "Hey there!" to her? I didn't think so. For the moment, she seemed content to be lost in a lonely world, but when she was ready to come out, I wanted there to be somebody there for her. Could I help make that happen, by simply wishing it to be so? There on that gorgeous beach, surrounded by sand and big, puffy clouds, the sound of water moving around my feet and the gulls overhead, everything seemed possible.

My roommate told me later one afternoon, as she waved a book at me, "It says here that the body is the *temple* of God —that we should keep it as pure as possible." She showed me the passage. I had read this somewhere before, or perhaps I had just *felt* it. It made a lot of sense. It was the type of idea you thought you'd learned in Sunday School or from your parents, and then realize you just always knew it; no one had actually told you. There were a lot of ideas like that that I was slowly beginning to think about. Edgar Cayce had said to one of his clients during a reading, "Laugh more, or you will get sicker." This makes sense, because if you're not happy, your body will get the message that you're not too thrilled with your life, and it will just say, "Okay, I've had enough; what's the point of keeping all these bodily organs and systems going if the life they provide is not enjoyed?" We think it incredible that Mr. Cayce could have pinpointed the problems of the people he saw, even though conventional medicine

remained baffled. Actually, he was just using common sense.
We all have grown out of touch with this ability to truly
"know" things, so his ability to draw on this power seems
incredible to us. He told another client, "This body does not
want to get well. Unless this body changes its way, it will not
get well." This is common sense. This is also macrobiotics.
Why is it that the simplest things in our lives are the most
difficult to understand? Most often we need a big jolt in order
to see them. We are very complacent, willing to let life roll
along, and even right by us, without noticing the simple
underpinnings which make it all possible. It's a wonderful
show of lights and talent, this life here on earth, complete
with huge, glittering stars in the sky and an endless variety
of terrain to dance upon. How, then, do we learn to get on
with the show?

I returned from Virginia, feeling calm and rested, to our
temporary home in Ferrisburg. The familiar walls of the
house made me remember how much I had needed this rest.
No longer did I feel as if the walls were closing in on me.
Rather, I began to see new possibilities—perhaps we should
hang a picture there, or move that chair just a little to the
right. I hoped I had learned a very important lesson, not to
ever again disregard my own needs for relaxation and care.
Because, I realized, if I did ignore them, nature would surely
take over and give me a permanent vacation, underground.

My mother had called while I was away. She was still living
just north of Boston, in the house Frank had built for her and
my father in 1947, just after we were married. Frank and I
were living nearby. We had begun our life together there;
he was building houses and I was working in area hospitals.
Our older children—Deborah, David, and Jeffrey—were born
and soon we decided to move our burgeoning family to Connecticut, where we continued, Frank building houses and I
producing babies—Dexter and Judith. I thought of my Mama,
sitting in her chair in the house I knew so well, crocheting,
reading, painting, talking with my sister Tarny, who lives

across the street, or with the neighbors. Mama's broken hip
had rendered her legs unsteady, although she gets around
pretty well with a cane. At eight-two, she was as sharp as
ever, and I had to be careful when I talked to her during those
days, that I did not reveal my situation to her. I did not want
her to know that I had cancer. When I called her, she said
she was just wondering what had made me decide to go on a
vacation all of a sudden like that. She said she thought it was
marvelous. She said I'd looked tired the last time she had
seen me. She said it was high time I did something for myself.
If she suspected I had cancer or any serious health problem,
she never let on. She must have known, though, because she's
very hard to fool. And this would have been a very big thing
for her to overlook. After all, we saw her at least every
month. It was strange and willful of me to try to keep my
illness from her. Besides, I know that a mother knows her
children in a special way. I know that if one of my children
were five thousand miles away and sick, I'd know it instinc-
tively, without being told. I suppose it was silly to try to
keep such a thing from my dear Mama, but it seemed important at the time.

I am grateful to Mama for the love of nature she has shown
me throughout my life and for my initiation into the spirit-
uality of life. In her simple, everyday way she had laid the
groundwork for my ability to self-reflect and to heal. I was
beginning to understand that we all have the ability to make
things turn out the way we want them to (in this case to
turn illness into health). Things don't just happen to us out
of the blue, don't just fall out of the sky onto our shoulders
as if we had no control over them. We make them happen.
I sensed that our bodies have within them the capacity for
the miracle of recovery from the malaise into which they have
fallen. I wanted to map the route back, by refusing the com-
plications of pills and surgery and by embracing a simple,
active life.

The days rolled by, with my wonderful family talking care

of me. Frank continued to fix up the house, slowing down at times when I would tell him, "I don't want to move, Frank, not right now." The thought of having to move, the way I was feeling, was just too much. I couldn't have managed it. I knew that when the renovation of the house was complete, it wouldn't be much longer after that that it would be sold and we would be on the move again. I just wanted some place to call home, now that I was sick. Frank, however, was faced with the practical matter of paying back $3,000 each month on the loans we owed. I don't know how he managed, but Frank was true to his word when he said we wouldn't move until I was better. We stayed in that house for one year after the mole on my arm had been removed. We had, all things considered, a normal family life during that time. I am sure being at home in a stable environment contributed greatly to my ability to recover quickly.

Judith and Melissa cooked for Frank and me. Melissa and Frank ate a ate a "normal" diet, and Judith stuck with me on the macrobiotic plan. She and I agreed that it tasted delicious, and she seemed to be getting stronger as a result of eating this way too. Gradually, I remember Frank and Melissa started eating differently also. Soon there was less beef on their plates and more fish and chicken. Melissa began leaving the butter off the vegetables she cooked for her father and herself, and I noticed she no longer drank a glass of milk with her dinner.

Julie and Jeffrey came over a lot. Nathan was growing quickly at that time. I wanted to reach my hand out to stop his rapid growth. I felt he was growing much too fast, faster than his old grandmother could appreciated. Always, I felt just a little too tired to hold him long enough, to talk to him, to tell his mother, Julie, how adorable he was. These last months of 1978 were my time to turn inward and try to recoup my strength. My energy had always been going out, to my children and their families, but I found I had just enough strength left to keep my own life going, and that was it. Always, in my mind, I was reaching out to my family. I hope they know that it troubled me to be so distant, but I couldn't think about it: I was trying to *survive*.

Our life during this time was quieter than usual. Melissa was finishing the winter term of her last year in high school. She often went off with her friends but hardly ever brought them home. She was very quiet then, keeping whatever worries she may have had to herself. It was good for her to have Judith there all the time. It took some of the responsibilities off her, and I am sure they must have talked sometimes about what was happening in the family. Long before I found out

Jeffrey and Julie Brown with their two sons Nathan (L.) and Nicki (R.) in front of their Vermont home.

I had cancer, ours was a difficult house to live in. It had been just Frank and Melissa and I. Frank and I were tense and upset about our financial situation at the close of the Kingsland Bay community. Looking back, I am sure it was not an easy situation for Melissa, with her parents arguing and upset much of the time. One nice result of my being sick was that Judith was with us and that the other children came over even more than usual.

Gradually, they too began cooking macrobiotic dishes and bringing them over for us to try. Slowly, our children's homes began to be influenced by the macrobiotic way of eating. As I began to improve, I saw that my recovery was having a strong influence on those around me. It was difficult not to be affected by what was happening, difficult not to see that what we are eating is profoundly affecting our lives. If their mother was improving with this diet, why couldn't they enrich their own lives by adopting a simpler diet? What I was beginning to see around me was a happier and a healthier family.

* * *

In late November, family from Vermont, Massachusetts, New Hampshire, and Connecticut gathered at the home of Frank's sister and brother-in-law for their annual pre-Christmas family party. I worried for days about what I would wear. Nothing fit me anymore, as I still weighed only one hundred pounds (Michio assured me the weight would come back in due time). I asked the girls what I could do to make myself look better, and they offered suggestions ranging from "wear a bright lipstick" to "forget about it and just smile." I was touchy about how I was going to look at the party because I hadn't seen most of the people who would be there since before I was diagnosed and since I had started on my new diet. I knew from comments some of the children made that the rest of the family was skeptical about what I was doing.

In some ways, I guess it is actually easier to go the medical route: to go to the hospital, have your treatments, and then pass away according to the life expectancy of your particular ailment. Following the accepted route insures that people around you will know how to act. They know when to bring flowers and when to offer sympathy and advice. You fit into an accepted pattern. But when you start going outside that "normal" structure, everyone becomes a little uncomfortable. It is as if one day it was decided that from now on the sun would rise only on Thursdays. People would get a little panicky and start doubting ideas they had always held as being "true." So, you become a little bit of an outcast when you follow a new path. It was okay with me. Besides, I had no choice. The accepted way of going to a hospital and taking my cancer like a "normal" person was not an option for me. I had never been afraid of being different. I do recognize, though, that this is a terrible decision for some people. To find themselves to be different from others is worse than having cancer, worse even, than dying.

I realize that the traditional way of health that has been forgotten by current medical practice is not the answer for everyone. I think, though, as more and more people benefit from traditional health care and their friends and relatives see them leading happier, more productive lives, the "other way" will not seem so strange any more and may even, one day, become a part of "the normal way." It is all a matter of what we are used to.

And, I realized as I walked up to the front door of Marion and Bill's home, wrapped in my wool overcoat, a hat pulled tightly around my ears, that I *liked* macrobiotics, that the food tasted good, that the philosophy was my own, and that, really, it was a part of my life now. I smiled brightly when Marion opened the door, and fell into the joy and the warmth of a hug with a woman I truly love and admire. It was going to be a happy Christmas.

The whole family was there, just as always. It was the one

time out of the year when we all got to see each other. I always liked seeing the family Frank and I had made surrounded by and blended together with this larger family. It made me feel that my children had roots, and that there would always be people who cared about them.

Bill raised a glass of beer to Frank and me from across the room and smiled. He made his way toward us and leaned over and kissed me on the cheek. He transferred his glass to the other hand and shook Frank's hand. The house was alive with Christmas decoration, lights in the windows, carved ornaments, holly along the stairway, a wreath on the door, and mistletoe in the alcove. There were little children running around everywhere, dressed in red velvets and green corduroys. Five of them I recognized, of course, as being my own grandchildren, and the others either had grown and changed so much since the year before that I didn't recognize them, or they were very new and this was their first family gathering and their first Christmas. Dexter grabbed Mary and kissed her under the mistletoe. Deborah came over and said I looked pretty and told me she had brought a casserole that I could eat. Jessie sprang out from behind her mother's skirts and hugged my knees.

The table was covered with rich foods, colorful and homemade, tempting dishes, set off by beautiful candles which flickered and winked. The windowpanes were iced over and reflected the color and light from the inside. I had been alone much of the time lately, and our house had been much quieter than usual, with people dropping over less and less. It was fun to be out, talking with everyone, holding the children in my lap, sitting back in my chair and watching the swirls of activity around me. I looked over at my mama who was sitting in a chair by the door. She would wonder why I was sitting in a chair like her, not being more active as I usually was. I started to get up out of my chair and looked back at her. It was at that moment that I came to a realization that was very comforting to me. I knew that she would accept whatever I was at that moment. If I were too tired to get up, she was not going to judge. It was a relief to let my guard down. I relaxed back in my chair and felt at peace.

Everyone there knew more or less that I had cancer. No one said anything about it, really. As a society, I think that when we use the word "cancer," we automatically assume that death is the natural result. It was much too happy a party to use the word "cancer." I turned back to Mama a few minutes later, and saw her surrounded by her great-grandchildren. She was whispering to them and they were listening carefully to her. I stretched my neck back as far as it would go, and I caught the words as she said them to the children, "Look for something beautiful, smell something wonderful," she stopped, looking around her and then continued in a conspiratorial tone, "then come tell me!" The

Deborah Brown with her son Jeremy, in her Vermont weaving store/studio.

children ran off, making circles all over the downstairs of the house. I smiled to myself and remembered the thousands of wonderful things my mama had given to me when I was a child.

We left early, before most of the other guests. I looked over at Frank behind the wheel of our car as he drove us home, and was happy to see him whistling and smiling to himself. Too often lately I looked over at him to find his face drawn toward his chest, sagging into a depth of unhappiness I could only guess at. He had had a lot to drink and had talked with everyone. He looked *much* better. This could have been an unhappy Christmas for us, my last—it was three months from the day the doctor had told me I had only six months more of life. I was still so tired these days that sometimes, at night when I went to sleep, I had the feeling that I might not wake up again. I developed a sense of gratefulness each morning as I awoke, for I was truly happy that I was here for another day . . . .

---

* ARE is a non-profit organization interested in parapsychology and making practical use of the Edgar Cayce readings.

6

Hitch your wagon to a star.
—Ralph Waldo Emerson

I SAW MICHIO KUSHI for the second time in January of 1979, more than four months after starting the macrobiotic diet. It seemed as if it had been much longer than that; it was as though it had always been a part of my life. Everyone was amazed at how much better I was in such a short time. I was eating downstairs now with the family every night and sometimes I helped the girls prepare dinner. I was not only eating macrobiotic food, I was beginning to learn how to cook it also! I saw Michio at a macrobiotic seminar he was giving, in the same building where I had gone to see Bill Tims that day, back in early September. I was faced with the same flight of stairs when we arrived but felt infinitely better about them this time than I had the last time. They still looked long and arduous, but not impossible. I wasn't prepared yet to run up them skipping every other step, but I was able to take them one at a time, at a pace a two-year-old would admire.

I saw Michio in a large room which was bare except for a long table and a few folding chairs. A couple of students sat off to one side, observing. Michio stood up and smiled when I came into the room. He shook my hand and offered me a seat opposite him. He looked at me carefully and smiled, nodding his head up and down. He looked away and then back at me again and smiled even more brightly after he seemed to confirm something. "You feel better." He was both asking me and telling me at the same time. I told him a little bit about what had been happening to me during the past four months.

I became aware that I was rattling on, so I stopped. He looked very pleased, as if I'd just given him a magnificent present. I wanted to tell him that he had told me, "*You* made it, and only *you* can change it" the last time I saw him, and that I *was* changing it, but it sounded a little arrogant to just come right out and say that *I* had done it and now *I'm* changing it. He seemed to know that I was mobilizing the right energy inside me to make the change. I really didn't have to say anything. He did ask me one question, however, and that was, "How are you?" We ask people this question all day long without really waiting for the response. I had the feeling, though, that my answer to this seemingly perfunctory question was very important, perhaps as an indication of how I was feeling about myself and what my reserves were concerning my ability to heal completely. It was a sign of how much faith I had in myself. I told him I felt great. And I did, relatively speaking.

Before I left, Michio told me I was 75 % better. I don't know how he put that percentage on my progress toward recovery, but he said it to me very carefully, and I believe that he in fact saw this much improvement in my health by observing changes in my face and hands. He told me I could now have fish once a week and that I could have a little dessert once in a while—something like applesauce. I left feeling inspired by the contact with him and had a renewed sense of my ability to heal.

After I left Michio, I went to see Bo-In Lee again, also for the second time. He too, was pleased with my progress. He told me to lie down on the floor again, as I had at the beginning of our first visit, and he showed me how I had equalized the right and left sides of my body by doing the exercises he had suggested. He showed me this by pointing to my toes, now pointing equally in opposite directions. Now, he said, I need to improve my energy flow. He told me that in my particular case I should alternate hot and cold showers every day and to rub my hands and feet with a rough cloth. He also changed my exercises. Suddenly I realized that he was no longer talking through an interpreter. It was then that I realized just what could be done in four months. He had learned English and I had recovered 75 % from cancer! This was much better than doing all the things I wanted to do for the last time, living out the end of my days in a matter of months.

I returned home feeling more courageous than ever. I continued on the diet—adhering to it strictly. Judith and Melissa continued to cook, and Frank and Melissa were coming around more and more to this new way of eating. I continued to get up early each morning, meditated, took my walk and did my exercises. Frank made oatmeal each morning as he had since the day after we were married. Things seemed to go along as if they'd always been this way.

Judith Brown (L.) on a recent trip east from her home in San Francisco and Melissa Brown (R.) visiting from Vermont, posed for this picture on the roof of their parents' apartment building next to the Charles River.

Slowly I began to be more and more interested in what Frank was doing around the house. I'd poke my head out the front door to ask him a question, or press my face to the windowpane trying to see him as he fixed the siding on the house. For the most part, I confined my new-found strength to indoor chores, helping the girls around the house, and I read a lot.

It was wonderful the way I suddenly had the time and the strength to read. I borrowed Michio's books from David and Debbie and read them hungrily. I had started on this diet knowing nothing of the philosophy behind it. I read Michio's *Book of Macrobiotics* and found the simple roots of the diet. I read his book on traditioned oriental diagnosis and was fascinated to learn some of the techniques available to read someone's health by looking at his face. I read exerpts from the Bible and I read *The Book of the Hopi*. My mother was always reading, and she recommended books for me too, mostly about ancient civilizations and about travel. My family got used to my carrying on and on about this Indian tribe and that civilization. Well, at least I was getting better, at least I had the *strength* to drive them crazy!

I remember one day, Melissa and Judith were making dinner. It must have been near the end of February, when everyone is just a little blue and waiting anxiously for the first signs of spring. It had been a long winter for us, a winter full of striving toward our happy goal of my release from sickness. We had all been together for months now. Mel called from the kitchen, "Judith, come here!" She continued when Judith came into the kitchen. "It says here six cups of water . . . doesn't that seem strange? I mean, you only need . . . ."

"Where are you looking?" Judith asked her.

Mel pointed to the cookbook on the table. "Right here," she pointed. I stood in the doorway and watched. Mel had one hand on her hip and the other hand on her head, holding her hair back.

"I'm sick and tired of rice," I told them. "I just can't eat another mouthful of rice. I'm not kidding."

"I know," Judith said.

"We know, Mother," Melissa said at the same time. "That's why I'm trying to make this . . . ."

"It must be a misprint, Mel," Judith said. "It'd get soggy if we use this much water. Don't you think?"

"Well, that's what I thought, but it's here in Lima Ohsawa's book[1]," she turned the cover back to show her sister as if to say, "how could this be wrong?" She had chicken and potatoes in the oven for herself and her father.

"Try using four cups of water and then add some while it's cooking if it gets too dry," Judith told her.

"I don't want to do anything . . . *wrong*, Judith," she stressed. It seemed she was referring to David's pressure that everything be cooked just right, or else.

"Just try it!" Judith said. "It'll be *fine*." She bounced out the door. "I'll be back in a few minutes."

"Let's see, Honey," I said, going over to where the book lay open. "This recipe?" I asked. "This recipe is for *couscous*."

"Yep," she said, measuring out some of the small yellow grains in a measuring cup. "You said you're sick of rice, so . . . ."

"Yes." I had made quite a scene the night before. I was so sick of chewing those little grains of rice over and over.

"We're just making the couscous, though, not the beans and the vegetables. I'm using the recipe for the proportions, but . . . ." Melissa measured out the four cups of water recommended by Judith, and put it in a pan to bring to a boil. "When the water boils, we pour in the couscous and simmer it for 4 or 5 minutes," Melissa said to no one in particular, as if confirming her ability to be doing this. "Right," she said, checking the recipe again. She stood watching the pan with the water in it, waiting for it to boil.

"Mel," I said, "how're things at school?"

"Okay," she said, fiddling with the cover to the pan.

"How did you do on your history paper?"

She looked at me funny, then washed the look off her face as she seemed to remember something. "That was six weeks ago," she said. "I got a B, *six weeks ago*."

"Oh," I said, "well, I knew I forgot to ask you, I'm sorry." She was still watching the pan with the water in it. She went over to the measuring cup of couscous and shook it, looking over the grains critically. Then she went back to the pan of water on the stove. "I hope this pan is big enough," she said.

"It looks okay," I said. I had sat down at the kitchen table.

"Yes," she began, and then stopped.

"Yes, but what?" I asked her, turning around to face her.

"It won't be big enough if I have to add more water, that's all," she said.

"So you'll transfer it," I said.

"I feel dumb getting all excited over the right pan, the amount of water, how much time, and everything else." She lifted her arms, then let them drop to her sides. "It's just *David*. He says that if I don't do everything *perfectly*, if I don't do it *just right*, if I . . . if I . . ." she lifted the lid of the pot containing the water, then put it back on. The water hadn't boiled yet.

"If you don't use the right pot, WHAT?" I shouted.

"If I don't use the right pot, you'll . . . you'll . . . you'll die!" she pounded her fist on the counter and whirled away from me, toward the stove.

"Melissa," I said quietly, "I am not going to die. Eventually I will die, but not until I am very old. And certainly not as a result of which pot you used to cook the couscous. Do you understand?" I got up and gave her a shake. "Cook the food any way you think is best. Use a lot of water or a little. Use that great big corn pot up there on the shelf, or bake it in the oven in a cast iron pan. Just cook it, dear, and I will gladly eat it." I kissed her and held her and could feel her breath twitter from her chest, like a bird.

I went out onto the front porch and breathed the cold February air. It doesn't get much colder than this, I thought, pulling my sweater around me. I looked up over the hills beyond and thought of warmer times at the beach, how the sun feels so hot overhead, beating down. It always intrigued me how Mother Nature could just toss out these extremes of weather at will, yet I knew it wasn't random at all. To a child, it seems so mean when the tide comes in and washes away the sandcastle he has built on a Sunday afternoon at the beach. It seems unfair, and he goes crying to his mother when the last turret has fallen, because he doesn't understand that the tide rises and falls according to pattern, not just in order to wreck his creation. Like disappointed children, we who do

Melissa riding our pony Cricket. She's about 12 years old here.

not understand the ways of nature are outraged by the damage
cancer does to our friends and relatives. However, if we
understand these ways of nature, we learn to build a castle
strong enough to withstand the tides, or we move the grand
house back out of the way, among the rose hips.

Judith came running up onto the porch, brushing by me and
on into the house. "What's the rush?" I wanted to ask her,
but realized as I had so many times during the last few months
that everyone else just *seemed* to be rushing around. In fact,
they were not. It was just that they were moving much faster
than *I* could. And also, at that moment, I felt almost ready
to be an active part of the family again. Mentally I was so
much better, but I was still weak, physically. So, I realized,
I was still watching life go by.

At dinner that night, Judith and I looked up at each other
as we ate the couscous. Or rather, as we tried to eat it. It
was very dry and kept getting caught in our teeth. Melissa
and Frank were concentrating on their own food, which
seemed to slide down their throats with hardly any chewing.
I set my fork down, leaned back in my chair and sighed.
Melissa looked up from her plate. "What's the matter,
Mother?"

"This is like trying to chew unpopped popcorn," I said.
"Here," I offered her my fork. "Try some."

She took some and made a face. "I guess it needed more
water."

"We should have followed the recipe," Judith said.

"Yeah," Melissa agreed.

"The *arame*[2] is terrific, though," she told her sister. I was
getting used to seaweed, but I couldn't, honestly, at that
point have said it was "terrific."

"I wouldn't eat that stuff," Melissa said. "Besides, I've
never eaten anything black before."

"Haven't you ever eaten licorice?" Judith asked her.

"Yes," she said in the sing-songy way she has when she

feels backed into a corner. "Yes," she repeated, "but that's different."

"How so?" Frank asked.

"It just *is*," she said.

Later that night Deborah called to say that she and David and Jessie would be coming by the next day. I told her about the fiasco with the couscous, and we laughed about it together. She told me to make barley or millet instead of rice if I get sick of it. She said not to worry, that I'd start wanting rice again soon. She also said that the recipes in Lima Ohsawa's book were pretty accurate. She had made nearly all of them at one time or another. I remembered the dog-eared copy of the book in her kitchen. It reminded me of my mother's copy of *Fanny Farmer* when I was a girl—how we'd pull it off the shelf and consult it for cookies, brownies and cakes! Often, when Mama and I were stirring the batter for some dessert, she would tell me how it was when she was a girl. I remember how often she told me about the sweets they had back then. Usually there were none, just an orange at Christmas, one for each child. She told me about the potato chips they made out of dulse[3]—so she had eaten seaweed when she was a girl. I was thinking about these old-fashioned ways which Mama had exposed me to as we followed the recipes, when Judith came in and told me David was on the phone.

"Hi, Dave," I said into the mouthpiece.

He told me I was impossible and dumb. Something about did I want to die and did I know what I was doing—it was my privilege, of course.

Ah, I suddenly realized, he's talking about the couscous. Deb must have told him. Couscous is listed under "Foods For Occasional Use," on my sheet from the East West Foundation. This means it isn't so good for me as some of the things listed under the heading, "Foods For Daily Use," but it wasn't *bad* for me. I told him, "David, I'm totally sick of rice, I can't eat another . . . ."

"Mother, this is not a matter of preference," he said. We're not talking about a red dress or a blue dress. You have to stick to your diet."

"I *am* sticking to my diet. I had a little bit of couscous tonight. It's not like I ate a slab of roast beef, dear."

He sucked in his breath. "Could you put Mel on, please, Mother?"

I told him she was out in the barn, even though she wasn't. I told him, "David, *don't worry*!"

He told me I could say that to everyone else but not to him, and hung up.

I tried to imagine the scene with Debbie after he got off the phone. I had to be good tomorrow when they came. I had to be very energetic so as not to start anything. I decided to go to bed right away in order to get as much sleep as possible. I didn't want to take a nap the next day while they were here. David gets so edgy when I do that, and then they all begin to argue . . . .

I couldn't believe my ears when I rolled over the next morning, looked at the clock which said eight o'clock, and heard David's voice downstairs. I had slept late, hoping to be fresh when the children came. "Darn it," I thought, as I rushed into my clothes. They were early—by about five hours.

I waited at the top of the stairs for the conversation to continue. I heard Melissa's voice but couldn't hear what she was saying. She sounded as if she wanted to cry, although I knew she wouldn't. Frank interrupted them. I heard David's boots leave the kitchen, and I hurried down the hall to the bathroom. I turned the water on to drown out the sounds of my children fighting about me. If anything would make me sick, it was that.

I washed my face and hands, brushed my teeth and painted a big red smile across my mouth. I was hurrying because I knew that David would be wondering why I was still in bed. He would start worrying because I'm always up by six o'clock. "Please," I said under my breath as I gripped the edge of the sink, "please let it be a calm day . . . just our nice family, together."

Downstairs, Frank and Melissa were in the kitchen eating oatmeal at the table. Neither one of them said a word or looked up when I came into the room. I ladled some oatmeal into a bowl.

"Hey Mother," David said as he same into the kitchen. He kissed me and peered into my bowl. "That's good stuff there," he said. "No one makes oatmeal the way Father does."

Frank looked up at him. "Well, we try, David."

"Yes, we do," Melissa said, using the entire range of the musical scale to achieve her response. "Thank you, Daddy," she said and hugged Frank from behind, around the neck.

"See you later, Pumpkin," he said and patted her arm.

David sat down in the seat she had just left. I was eating my cereal standing up, as I used to do years ago in our house in Woodstock, when the children were little. "Where are Deb and Jessie?" I asked.

David waved his hand toward the door. "Outside," he asid, "Jessie's riding Silver." Frank got up and poured himself another cup of coffee.

"You need some help with the roof today, Dad?" David asked.

"Yeah, I suppose," Frank answered his son. "We'd better get to it today." He looked up at the ceiling. "That thing isn't going to hold if we get rain." His tone sounded like *he* wasn't going to hold through the day.

"Oh, c'mon, Frank, it isn't as bad as all that," I told him —I remember saying things like this at that time. I was trying so hard to sound cheery and strong, I must have sounded very odd sometimes.

"That thing's a mess up there," Frank reminded me. He ran his fingers through his hair and then shook his head. "I'm sixty years old," he said, "and I'm still crawling around on top of someone else's roof so we don't get wet."

At that moment Jessie ran through the door and bumped

into Frank. "Grandpa!" she said, the words spilling from her tiny mouth. She was excited about having just ridden the horse. I couldn't hear what she was saying, but it didn't matter, because suddenly a heavy mantle had been lifted from our house. She watched as Frank engulfed her mother in a hug, then followed her grandpa outside. Debbie went over to the basket they had brought from home, filled with onions and fresh kale, which David had brought in from their car and put under the sink. "It still looks pretty good," I told her. "The kale doesn't look any worse for storage," I said. "Thank you, dear."

I was so grateful to have my family around me and thankful for the fresh foods they provided from their gardens. I looked out the window over the sink and saw Frank circling the house. The corners of his mouth were turned down, and his fists were resting on his hips. Jessie was reaching for his hand . . . .

[1] *The Art of Just Cooking*, by Lima Ohsawa, originally published by Autumn Press. and now by Japan Publications, completely revised and expanded under the title of *Macrobiotic Cuisine*.

[2] sea vegetable

[3] sea vegetable

7

Nothing endures but change.
—Heraclitus

AND SO THE DAYS PASSED, as did the seasons, and
suddenly one morning my heart felt lighter as I saw
that we were coming into spring . . . .
During the spring my mama visited us a lot. She'd sit in a
chair on the porch while I walked over the fields in front of
the house, picking flowers and waving them in the air to her.
We'd both call out the names of the flowers together. I
cherish these "walks" we took together that spring, she in
her chair on the porch and I walking through the tall grass.
We counted sixteen varieties of wild flowers right outside
the house. As I admired the new blossoms, I felt something
green rising within me: something new, something fresh,
and something whole. Once again I was a little girl, scamper-
ing after a butterfly on a Sunday afternoon, and there was my
mama, watching me from her chair, with wisdom and comfort
and a ready laugh. She never said anything about my cancer.
She was simply there.

* * *

Later in the spring we decided to take a trip to Florida. It had
been a hard winter and Florida beckoned to us like crystal
clear water in the middle of the desert. Frank and I flew to
Tampa, while Judith and Melissa drove our car down. We
spent the next few days driving around, exploring. The
weather was very cold, and we had a lot of trouble finding

places to eat. We stayed in an efficiency apartment for three days so that we could cook, but all in all it became clear that it is very difficult to travel, while adhering to this strict diet. As long as we stayed in the room with the kitchen, we were all right, but when Judith and Melissa flew back home and Frank and I drove the car back, we had a terrible time going from town to town, from health food store to health food store looking for something I could eat. As far as restaurants went, sometimes I could find a plate of vegetables I could eat (if I got to the cook before butter had been put on them) but no rice at all. When my supply of food we had cooked at the motel was gone, I just had to content myself with being hungry until we got home. To make matters worse, Frank wouldn't eat if I couldn't. If we went into a restaurant and there was nothing for me, he would turn around and walk out. So, we were *two* hungry people. When we stopped at a natural food store (there weren't very many back then), I was able to get rice cakes to stave off my hunger. Between the bad

Virginia (R.) with her Mother, Adelaide Marion Bratt

weather in Florida and the depressing trip home, it was an awful time—not much of a vacation, at all.

I was grateful to get home and smell food on the stove, prepared by the girls. I was so thankful for my plate of food that day, and so appreciative of the wholesome quality of it, compared to the food I had seen while we were on the road. It is indeed difficult to travel as one might normally when on a strict diet. But then, I smiled to myself as I thought of it, maybe that just means it would be best to stay home until one has dealt with one's illness sufficiently before venturing out into the world again to meet other challenges there. We have to be secure in our own well-being before we can stand up to the rigorous demands of the outside world. We *need* home when we are sick. Perhaps we should stay there and be happy we have the comfort of a place to call home—until we are ready. I was being a little fresh with myself to just wander off like that and expect to be able to take care of myself as I should. The treatment I was undergoing for my cancer was deceptively subtle. Although I was home (not in a hospital) and our family life was normal, I was still undergoing very specific treatment. It was important for me to stick to the regimen of the diet, just as it would have been necessary for me to follow the doctor's orders for taking medication.

A well person would not have the same problems I had with traveling, while eating in a macrobiotic way. This is even more true today than it was back then in 1979. My problem was that within the macrobiotic diet I had to be particularly careful of certain foods. I had found, once again, the value of our home and our family.

Spring eased into summer, and things stayed pretty much the same for our family. My condition continued to improve. I began to follow Frank around the house while he did the repairs, nails in his mouth. He always had an air of competence about him. He was putting the house back together again piece by piece. In doing so, he never lost sight of the true character of the house. He made certain that the essence did not get lost in his repair work. While I was healing my body, ridding it of the symptoms which we call illness, in fact I was healing my very core. It was the same with the house. Frank was true to the design of the house, the people who had lived there before us, the things it had been through, while infusing it with renewed strength to hold up its wooded sides and form shelter with its broad roof. When Frank had finished renovating a house, you had the feeling it was really what it was supposed to be. This is a lot like macrobiotics. It is not the exterior that is important, but rather what is going on inside, allowing the structure to maintain space for the hopes and dreams held inside. Frank could have scraped the old paint from the house and slapped on a pretty color; he could have replaced the crumbling bricks in the chimney and he could have put a new door on the house. But this wouldn't have changed the plumbing, the wiring, the rotting supports, and the leaks in the basement. It wouldn't have *changed* anything; it just would have made the house *look* better. In fact, the house would have still been in the same danger of falling down. I couldn't help seeing parallels between what Frank was doing with the house and what I was doing with my body. I realized that it is not until the inside changes—not until that is fulfilled or understood, or allowed to be expressed, that true cure takes place.

I pattered around the house, smiling more now. I could hear Frank up on the roof—bang! bang! The sounds were so familiar. I heard them in my ears, felt them in my heart. I knew my body was repairing itself in much the same way; with the same care, certainty, competence, and dogged assuredness. We were putting our lives back together again.

Melissa had graduated from high school that spring and was working up in Burlington as an usher in a local summer stock theater. She really enjoyed it, and I am sure it was a relief for her to get away from home every day, although she was still living with us. I was happy she had less of the responsibility for the house now, and glad to realize that I was able to take on more and more of the responsibilities of the house myself. Julie and Jeffrey moved to Cornwall, Vermont, near Middlebury. They were still nearby, but they weren't around quite so much as they were before. Julie was expecting their son Nicky, who was born the following fall. Dexter and Mary were working on their recording studio. I went down to see their place as I got better. They had taken an old house and rebuilt and redecorated it. Frank did the fireplaces and I helped Mary with the painting.

Our oldest, Deb, called Frank one night, early in August. I didn't know of their conversation until many months later. Frank had told me that she had called just to ask how I was doing, and that she was getting her own life back together again, after the breakup with her husband. Frank didn't tell me the rest of the conversation, however, which I learned later. It seemed that Deb had been to a party the night she called Frank, and had overheard a conversation there about me. Someone was saying to someone else how awful it was about me, how sick I was, and how they had been given the impression that there was no hope for me. This shocked Deb because she had had no idea how sick I had been, as she was caught up in her own troubles at the time and was careful not to upset me by including me in them. She knew I was sick, but she didn't realize how grave it had been in the beginning. She hadn't been there during the process of my recovery. Frank explained to her that it *had* been very bad, and the doctor's prognosis had been terrible a year ago. He told her the diet was working for me and I was much better. He felt that I was out of danger now. He told her not to worry.

I remember being glad that Deb had called to see how I was. I missed her around the house. We had always been so close, and I felt cut off from her. I know it couldn't have been any other way, and it was a difficult time for all of us. In the warmth of summer, I was able to open my eyes wide and look for miles over the fields in front of our house. I loved the trees, the hills, the sky, the birds, the breeze over the blue-green grass. I loved the feeling of strength I had running through me. I loved the fact that Frank could have told one of our children not to worry, that "Mother is going to be fine . . . ."

I did a lot of the painting on the inside of the house. While I couldn't paint a whole house, as I used to, I was doing very well and my help with the house was very much appreciated. It was little things like this and like making dinner for everyone that made me a part of our family again. Even more than these physical things, I began to feel my family's needs again. I realized how much the children needed me to delight in their successes and comfort them in their failures. I felt I was there again to do those things. I still tired easily, but I wasn't as inward as I had been during the winter. I found myself reaching out more and more to the work that needed to be done and to my children and my husband.

I was going back to doing a lot of the things I had done before I got sick, but there was definitely a difference. I had not fully regained my strength, by any means, but even these initial stages of getting back into the flow of our family life were different. I realized carefully, that *I* was different. Not only did I have the perspective on life that a person gets when she has a brush with death, but I felt that, intrinsically, I had changed. I had become more easy going and I had become more appreciative of the little things in life. I realized, happily, that I was no longer irritated so much by things that didn't matter.

What I had undergone during the past year, in addition to an incredible alleviation of my cancer, was a change in life-style. It seemed to me that the cause and the way to recovery from sickness were one and the same thing: lifestyle. I had been leading a very unhealthy lifestyle, amid the natural Vermont landscape in which I had lived for twenty years. I had lost my connection with the natural world, becoming more

and more alienated from it. It made me think how easily
people living in the cities could become estranged from the
natural order of life. If I could do it in the magic of the country, city dwellers could let this connection slip away with
barely a second thought.

During the past months I had learned to respect the ways
of nature because I wanted to stop offending that which gave
me health and happiness. I wanted to live. I felt at peace with
whatever would happen to me, for I felt that I had changed
my lifestyle so that my body could have the opportunity to
be whole again. You see, it was *my choice*, all along. Sometimes, when we are gravely ill, we are too sick to see another
path. I am very grateful to have been able to maintain enough
spirit to see another way.

I used to eat a lot of eggs, for example. I told everyone,
including myself, that I ate them because I *loved* them. It was
common knowledge in our family, that "Mother loves eggs."
To be honest, I don't really know whether I loved eggs or not.
I ate them because they were easy to make. It wasn't any
more complicated or interesting than that. It was just con-
venient. With a large, growing family, you never have much
time to yourself, but I was taking it to extremes. Perhaps I
just didn't *want* much time to myself. Perhaps I was afraid of
what I might find if I began to look inward. So, I devoted all
of my energy to everyone around me. In fact, I don't think
Frank and I ever went out together, just the two of us,
except once a year, on our anniversary.

My energy was constantly going out to our children, their
friends, our friends, patients at the hospital. When, I wonder,
did I ever recharge my battery? I believe we do with our lives
what we want. I believe this is what I wanted at that time.
But when I got sick, I found I needed to take what my family
wanted to give *me*. I had no more energy to give out, and if
I wanted to rejuvenate, I had to learn to take from them. I
had to make the choice, whether to live or whether to die.
I had abused myself to the point where my body was stopping

me in my tracks and asking me, "Hey, Lady, do you want to live—or don't you?" It was really just that simple. And if I had relied on the doctor's proposed therapies, I think I would have been letting him answer that question for me. It would have been out of my hands and into his, and I don't think any doctor in the world could have turned that question around to face me in a way that I could have answered with any degree of strength in the affirmative. No one could have. I had to do it myself.

It was at this time, late in the summer of 1979, as my strength returned, as I began to interpret what had happened to me, and as I felt welcomed back into life, that I realized that macrobiotics had become part of my life. As a nurse, I have been trained to view treatments as being something outside of ourselves—a pill, a surgical procedure, or a physical therapy that is applied to the problem and then withdrawn when the patient is better. However, I came to realize that the dietary changes I had made in order to rid myself of cancer had become changes in my way of life, changes which enhanced my life, overall. I knew I wasn't all better yet, but I felt better than I had since—and I say this with a lot of reserve—really, since I was very young, maybe even since I was in my early twenties. The world looked fresh and new to me again. To be sure, being on the edge of death and then being restored to life gives one a sense of appreciation, but there was more. Today, six years later, I still feel that same sense of wonder each morning as I wake up. It had been many, many years since I could respond to my mother's direction to, "Go find something beautiful, hear something wonderful . . . ." I would tell myself that only children feel this way. Adults have seen too much of the ways of the world to enjoy such an enthusiastic view of life. I was wrong. I found that as I started to eat whole, unprocessed foods in amounts and proportions suitable to my needs and that were selected from the bountiful offerings of the land near our home, this happy feeling returned.

Macrobiotics does not solve anything, but it does relieve that desperate feeling that there are no reasons for our suffering. It takes you by the hand and gently nudges you toward the door. It is up to you whether or not you decide to kick the door open. If you want to go through the door, you will find that you have the strength to do so. This, anyway, has been my experience.

As I became more useful around the house I began to notice certain things. One night while I was washing our dinner dishes I saw that there was a greasy ring around the sink. I couldn't imagine what could have caused it, as I sprinkled cleanser over the sink and scrubbed with a sponge. Frank and Melissa had stopped eating red meat months ago, and I could only remember that sort of fatty ring resulting from a dinner back when we put steak or hamburgers on the table. But now everyone was watching what we ate. I looked over into the garbage pail and saw the ckicken bones I had put there, from Frank's plate. I remember the exact moment when, as I held the sponge poised over the sink, I had realized that chicken must have many of the same fatty qualities as red meat. But everyone says that chicken is such a lean food! Well, I guess it is, compared to beef. I continued to scrub the sink. I was using a blue sponge and it was turning yellow. It may be leaner than steak, I thought to myself, but I decided to talk to Frank about not having it so often. He was eating chicken just about every night then, as he had stopped eating other things. He was not quite ready to go on a totally macrobiotic diet, and yet he knew that a lot of what we had eaten all during our lives had not been very good for us. So, he was taking the middle road. I wasn't sure this was much better than eating steak—I thought again about the greasy chicken bones and shuddered.

At any rate, I'm sure I was hyper-sensitive about it because I was on such a strict diet and my view was somewhat narrowed, but I was very concerned about the health of my family and friends, and also people at large, as I began to live the difference that what you eat can make in the way you feel and in the way you resist degenerative disease.

One thing that struck me as being important, as I watched my family switch gradually to a more natural diet; it isn't so much what we are omitting from our meals that is so important, as it is what we are *actually eating*. I was told not to eat meat, milk, cheese, butter, and eggs, but I was told in far greater detail what *to* eat—whole grains, beans, and vegetables, and the rest.

So much of what we hear today revolves around what *not* to eat, it's a wonder anybody knows what to eat any more. I went back to cleaning my sink—the ring was nearly gone. Food that sticks to your sink sticks to your body and gums it up, same as your drain. It's really just a simple house-cleaning problem. For the stopped-up sink we use Drano, and for the person clogged and hardened with fat and tumors we use surgery. I was pleased with the way the sink looked after I'd scrubbed it. I turned to wipe my hands on a dishtowel and felt a sense of accomplishment.

8

To travel hopefully is a better thing
than to arrive.
                              —Robert Louis Stevenson

I WENT TO SEE MICHIO KUSHI for the third time the same
week we moved out of the house in Ferrisburg, toward
the end of August, 1979. David and Deborah drove me to
Boston and waited at the Seventh Inn Restaurant while I took
the subway out to Michio's house in Brookline. It was a hot,
humid day, but it didn't seem to bother me. The subway car
was full so I stood, hanging on to an overhead loop, watching
the trees go by the windows of the trolley car. I felt bouncy,
looking down at my sneakers. They were new. Like a child,
I was admiring them, rolling back and forth on the balls and
heels of my feet, testing their spring.

Deborah had said, "*David*, how can you let Mother ride
the subway out there!" Then to me she had said, "Of course,
we'll take you all the way." But David had prevailed, saying
that I was fine and could manage by myself. He was right,
and furthermore I was tired of being a burden to everyone. I
wanted to take the subway; it made me feel carefree and
young.

I walked the mile or so from the trolley station to Michio's
house. He lives in a beautiful section of town and, as I was
early, I explored some of the backroads near his home. It was
hard to believe another fall and winter were upon us—seasons
I wasn't supposed to be here to enjoy. Well, I thought as I
looked up at the open sky, "I'm here!" It was a quiet thought,
a strong and enduring thought, and I was glad.

Michio greeted me in his characteristic way, by carefully looking into my face and asking me how I felt. I was aware that I was revealing myself to him. He smiled and took my right hand and poked at the palm with his thumb. "See," he said, "there are still bumps." I felt the heel of my palm where he was pointing. "Still a little bit there," he added, "but much better."

We talked for a little while. I told him how happy I was that I was getting well and that I wanted to find out more about why and how it was happening. I said I was thinking about coming to Boston to study at the Kushi Institute where, I felt, I could learn more about macrobiotics.

Michio reiterated how much better I was and told me to eat very strictly for the next three months. In some ways I felt a little defeated by what he said. Secretly, I had been hoping that he would tell me I was all better. I have always pushed myself to do things well, quickly, and with a minimum of fuss. I had come to feel I could deal with anything. Now I felt I had dealt with my cancer in my usual competent and efficient manner. Well, I guess it was time for me to be humbled. I thought I had licked this thing, forgetting for the moment the reasons why I had gotten sick—the lack of respect for my own needs. Probably, I really wasn't ready to be completely well yet. I wanted to get well because that would have seemed miraculous and exciting, but actually what I needed was a calm, careful recovery. These were qualities which I was learning. For the first time I was really considering the idea of a healthy future. My symptoms were going away—in fact many of them were gone, and I had the feeling of having been renewed. But I realized, after seeing Michio this time, that I was not yet fully recovered because that something way inside me which he had touched during our first visit had not yet fully changed.

In the weeks that followed, I often felt the bumps in my hands. They served as a reminder that I am related to everything and that I can't pretend to be anything I'm not. I couldn't tell Michio, "Don't worry," and smile and have him believe me. The body doesn't lie to someone who understands the language.

I returned home, chastened. Frank was busy with the last minute details of the house. We were moving in two days. We would be going to the small cabin my family shared by a lake in New Hampshire. After that, we had no idea where we were going. Frank had gotten a good offer for the house; it was ready to be sold, and we really couldn't wait any longer, as our loan payments became due, month after month. The day we left the house in Ferrisburg is inscribed on my memory as if each moment were organized and pasted into a huge, non-yellowing scrapbook. So much had happened during our year in that house. Our lives had turned a corner. As I was finishing up some last minute packing that day, Frank was calling to me:

"Everything's in the trunk, Jinny," he called up the stairs. I was checking under the beds and came upon a box of papers under the bed Melissa had used. I dragged the box out from under the bed and began looking through the papers. There was a deed from one of the houses we'd built in Woodstock, a receipt from the hardware store for a power drill, Geoffrey's birth certificate, a letter from my father . . . I decided we'd have to take the box along.

"Everything fit in the trunk, Honey," Frank repeated, his hands on his hips as he stood in the doorway to what had been Melissa's room. Then, noticing the papers strewn over my outstretched legs he said, "What is all this?"

"We must have saved them for *some* reason," I said more to myself than to him. "This is Debbie's writing," I said, as I pulled out a sheet of paper with childish writing on it.

"Could be any of them," Frank said, shifting from one foot to the other.

"I remember," I said. "It's Debbie's." I laid the paper down on my knee and stared off into space.

"Come on," Frank leaned over me and the box. "We'll

put it on the back seat of the car."

"You got everything in the trunk?" I turned around to look at him for the first time.

"There isn't that much, Jinny," he said. "Three suitcases, a couple of boxes, and our coats."

"Hmmm," I thought, we weren't leaving with much in the way of material things. Frank scooped up the box of old papers and took it downstairs. I straightened up and looked out the window. So, this had been Melissa's view for the past year. I hoped she had been comforted by the wide open fields and the hills beyond. She had watched the countryside turn from brightly colored to bare gray and white, to vibrant green. Had she wondered if I would be giving up the view from my window for good? If she did, it never showed.

I remember her standing at this dresser the night before she left for her new apartment in Burlington. She was brushing her long brown hair, arching her back to get at the underside. She said she had never worried about me. "*You* never got upset," she said, "so *I* never did. I had complete faith in you. You said you'd do it and I believed you." She had put the brush down on the dresser and opened her suitcase lying on the floor. "Especially in the beginning," she continued, "when David was telling me what to do. I didn't have *time* to think about it. He said, "Do it this way, or *else* . . . . Mother won't be around any more if you don't'." She had taken her sweaters out of the drawer and tossed them into the suitcase. Then she had stopped, picking at her finger. "I guess we all trusted David—and you. We didn't have time to think about it. We just did it. And then you started getting better right away, and there was no reason to think about your not getting well, because you already were." I had pulled her close to me and watched our reflection in the mirror over the dresser. "Oh Mom . . . ," she had held me around the neck, and I had felt the fullness of her love—it had felt light and airy, and I had thought I would burst with happiness.

Frank called from downstairs again. Was I ready to leave?

"I'm ready," I said under my breath. I got into the front seat of the car and closed the door. Frank leaned in through the open window. "I'm glad we're leaving this place," he said.

"Me, too, Frank," I said, "me, too." Frank went back into the house one more time to lock the door. I thought about my first walk after I was sick, running out of the house, hearing the screen door bang behind me, feeling the warm, soft air fill me like a hug. I yawned and smiled at Frank as he got into the car. "We're a good team, Frank," I said.

"Yup," he said, backing out onto the road.

I wish I could think back on that house with better feelings, but we had dumped so much grief there. We had gotten rid of a lot of things we didn't need any more. Perhaps we had spent the time in that house separating the important things from those we could live without. We had been brought back to the essentials, and we were redefining our lives in those terms.

And besides, we had a lot to look forward to. We drove along the same road Melissa and I had traveled that day north for the results of the biopsy. We had come south with the bad news and planted it in the yard of the house we had just left. We sowed what we had planted, a fresh crop came in, full and lush because of how we took care of that garden and life went on. We had had a choice, we had faced it, and now we were moving on. I do believe there was a choice, whether to give up or whether to move on. We had decided to continue . . . .

* * *

It was very humid as we drove to the cabin by the lake. When I was a little girl, my mother, father, sister, and I had often come to this lake for a vacation. The lake is at the center of many of my fondest childhood memories. It is also where I had met Frank, when we were teen-agers. Although we didn't see each other for a few years after our first meeting, our love for the lake was indicative of many of the values we have in common. Soon after we were married, my mother and father had bought a small piece of land by the lake and Frank had built for them this house where we would spend the next two weeks while we decided what to do next.

I was sitting at the edge of the dock, dangling my feet in the water. I remember doing this when I was a little girl. I loved the way the sun caught the drops of water on my toes. The sky was very blue, making the water look bluer than usual. Frank came up behind me and put his hands on my shoulders. We both looked out over the shimmering lake. After a few minutes he sat down next to me, wrapping his arms around his knees.

I think we should do this more often," I said, scooping a handful of water and shaking it. Droplets of water danced on the surface, then plunged beyond.

"What I wish," he said, drawing his fingers through his graying hair, "is that we had already done this many times."

Frank with grandson Nathan

I was beginning to notice deep lines around his eyes.

"It doesn't matter," I told him, leaning against his knees. "Nothing matters, but this." I spread my arms out, then relaxed with a smile. I tried to imagine Frank here by himself, had I died six months ago. It was hard for me to focus on a picture of him here, alone on the the dock, without me. I knew that the children wouldn't have left him alone, but somehow, even surrounded by them, Frank would have looked lost. We were always together, it had always been that way —it was *supposed* to be that way, and it always would be.

I patted his arm and told him I was thinking of going to Boston to study. I told him I wanted to know more about what had happened to me. I had followed the diet, but I knew there must be more to it. I wanted to understand the principles behind what had happened to me. I could feel intuitively what was going on, but I knew there was more to it. This seemed like a good time to go, if I were ever going to. Frank had work in Vermont, and we were unsure about where to live. I knew he could stay with the children and I could stay with Mama. Deb and David had mentioned they might hire me at Erewhon*, in Boston, for part-time work.

I felt bad about leaving Frank, but I explained to him that all my life all I ever wanted to do was help people. If there was a general application for macrobiotics in people's lives, I wanted to understand it and help people learn about it. I felt there was a lot to discover in Boston. Also, I wanted a chance to be with other people who were eating in a macrobiotic way. I was so close to Boston where, it seemed, it was all happening, it would have been frustrating not to go there and find out more. Besides, now that I was feeling so much better, I felt it was time to try to give something back. I needed to participate.

Frank agreed that it was a good idea for me to go. He, too, was interested in how we might help other people benefit from the dietary plan. "If you really want to go," he said, "it's okay with me. Just take care of yourself," he said, his

tone rising. "You're not out of the woods yet, you know."
He looked at me severely. "Michio said 'be very strict.' "
I sensed that he wished he could think of a good reason for
me *not* to go. He took my face in his hands and kissed me.
I felt like a precious jewel that had been discoverd beneath
the lake instead of the skinny, sickly, past-middle-aged woman
that I was.

We threw pebbles into the water until the sun had been
swallowed up by the trees on the opposite shore. We crossed
arms as we stood up and walked back to the cabin feeling
tousled and tired and optimistic about the future.

---

* Natural foods company started by Michio and Aveline Kushi that has
set the standards for natural foods throughout the world.

9

Hold fast to dreams
For if dreams die
Life is a broken-winged bird
That cannot fly.

Hold fast to dreams
For when dreams go
Life is a barren field
Frozen with snow.
                    —Langston Hughes

WHEN OUR TWO WEEKS AT THE LAKE WERE OVER, I left for Boston. The day I waved good-bye to Frank and the children was sunny and still mild for early September. The car windows were open all the way and my hair blew as I stepped on the accelerator and headed south.

For the first time in over a year, I was alone. While I had needed my family during this past year, I sometimes resented my dependency on them. This sounds ungrateful, but I think, in a way, it was an assertion on my part that I was getting well. It was a relief to be going away, even though I would miss everyone, because it was as though I could simply leave the cancer back in Vermont. Boston was free of the kinds of associations I had built up in Vermont, and I felt I could make a fresh start. When it was time to come home, Vermont would be aired out, like a musty old house that was made liveable again by leaving the windows open and beating the draperies and upholstery with a stiff broom.

When I got to Mama's house in Reading later that afternoon, she was sitting in a chair on the front porch, waiting for me to arrive. She called to me as I got out of the car. I ran up the steps and kissed her. She looked at me and told me I looked "good!" She said it with a combination of relief and skepticism. As she had found out more and more about the kinds of foods I had been eating, she had begun to worry, even though it was so apparent how much better I was. I knew she was reading a lot about the subject, trying to relate it to the extensive understanding she had of ancient cultures. I had to laugh, Mama could talk about Eskimos, Aztec Indians, African Bushmen, and Druids as if they were her next door neighbors. At eighty-two, she had a more open mind than most people a quarter of her age. Yet, in my case, I could feel her worrying that I had refused all medical treatment, for I had finally told her I had cancer.

Within her broad cultural understanding, she found a sound basis for the macrobiotic diet, and came to support it, at least from the point of view of healthy living. She was still committed to her white bread and jam and would defend it by saying, "Look at *me*; it hasn't done *me* any harm!" But she did see the merit in it, even if she couldn't fully support the way I was using diet to recover from cancer.

She lifted herself part way out of her chair as I kissed her. Mostly in her chair, her influence and vivacity extended to the people and space around her.

It was good to go inside and feel the security of the house surrounding me, like an old quilt around my shoulders. Here, I felt protected from the aggressive world outside. I had often felt this way in Vermont, and that is why Frank and I had loved living there so much. But lately I had felt less and less comfortable there. I felt Vermont had let me down—after all, I had gotten cancer there, in the most beautiful, most natural environment in all of America. Yet I knew that the pollution that had caused my illness was not the fault of Vermont at all, nor the responsibility of any outside factors. Surely the contaminant which contributed to my illness came from within myself.

I tossed my suitcase down on my bed and went back outside to talk with Mama. My sister Tarny and her daughter, Karen, were crossing the street from their house. "We saw your car and couldn't wait to come over," Tarny said as they walked up the driveway. She was holding a pie plate out in front of her. "It's apple," she said, extending it to me. "I figured you could have it since you're eating applesauce." I thanked her and wondered what else was in the pie beside apples. It was the love in the pie, of course, that was the most important ingredient, but I still had to be very careful. I was in "the real world" now. Judith and Melissa weren't in the kitchen any longer catering to my needs. It was time for me to make my way alongside the rest of the world, where most people don't have an understanding of the refinements of the diet I was on. I lifted a corner of the foil covering the pie and peeked in. "Thanks, I'll love it," I told my sister, then hugged and kissed her and Karen. It certainly was good to be with them.

That night I made dinner for the four of us. I made miso soup, brown rice, a mixture of carrots, squash and onions, steamed broccoli, and black beans. Mama, Tarny, and Karen also had chicken. They were very nice about the food I cooked. They liked the soup and the beans, and even the rice.

But it was unbelievable to them that this type of diet was helping to cause my improvement. They became philosophical about it. They supported me, said they were behind me, no matter what. And they tried to understand. Throughout my stay in Boston, they were always asking questions, listening, always wanting to know more about it.

Mama's house was filled with plants. Her house is a living example of her creativity and patience. As older people age, a sense of the slowing down of life seems to creep through a house. Not so with Mama's house. Every time I'm there, the house seems to surge with life. It seems to breathe, its walls moving in and out rhythmically with the hopeful endeavors going on inside.

I looked at the picture of my father on the mantle and wondered what he would have thought of my new way of life, had he been living. He wouldn't have said very much, of course; that was his way. Probably deep down he would have understood. It was a kind of discipline, this dietary regimen, and he could relate to an orderly way of life. In fact, I think he might have been impressed that I was introducing some sense of regulation into my life.

I called Erewhon the next morning and made an appointment to see about a job. I also signed up for classes at the Kushi Institute. I would be enrolled in Level I. I did some work around Mama's house that day. I can't help reflecting on how lucky I am to have such a wonderful family—my mother, sister, husband, children, grandchildren, everyone. I remembered patients in the hospitals where I had worked who lay in their beds for days without a visitor. How could life be worth living without people who care about you?

I started work as a secretary at Erewhon's warehouse in Somerville. My hours were 7:00 A.M. until 3:00 P.M. I came home after work, made dinner, then drove forty minutes to Brookline to attend classes from 7:00 P.M. until 10:00 P.M. This was my schedule Monday through Friday. It was a full schedule, but I was determined to make it work. On weekends, I got into the routine of driving back to Vermont to be with Frank. We stayed with the children.

They served macrobiotic meals at the warehouse, and the work wasn't overly strenuous. There were many days when I simply sat on the floor while I did my filling. I was too tired to stand, and no one said anything about it. David and Deborah had told me about how Erewhon had been started. They said Michio and Aveline Kushi gave lectures on macrobiotics at night. Only a small group of people attended them at that time (as compared to the hundreds of people who come to their lectures now). Sometimes only one or two people showed up. Michio and Aveline started bagging brown rice, which they sold to people who attended the lectures. This was almost twenty years ago. As people became more and more interested in natural foods, they decided to sell wholesome foods in a more organized way. They decided to call their endeavor "Erewhon," after Samuel Butler's utopian novel.

The courses at the Kushi Institute were wonderful, and it was good to be surrounded by macrobiotic people. I learned so much during those three months of study from the courses and from talking with the people I met in my classes. Some people were there because they were sick, others were there because they wanted to learn all they could before beginning to help others with macrobiotics in other parts of the world. It impressed me how many people were from other countries. I hadn't realized what widespread interest there was in this way of life. The classes we took were in cooking, the oriental art of physiognomy, philosophy, macrobiotic healing, and we had lectures given by Michio.

During one lecture that Michio gave I remember he had just flown in from a holistic seminar in Toronto. He told us that all during the two-day seminar about what to eat and what not to eat, he was concerned that there had been no mention of the spirit. He said that the spirit is the most important aspect of health and an integral part of the healing process. He said we need to believe in something larger than ourselves—a god or whatever makes sense to us in terms of our own religious and philosophical backgrounds. I was glad to hear him say this, because during my own recovery I had felt very strongly that what I ate was very important, but, indeed, what I was thinking and feeling was at least as important as what I was eating.

It was thrilling to hear Michio say things I had read in his books. The ideas were so much more alive when heard this way, when shared with others in the class. There was an exchange of ideas, making the whole experience so much more valuable than simply reading all by yourself. It seems that he synthesized the essence of different cultures into one cohesive, common sense whole. The point of his message, I felt, was that although we all have our differences, the traditions we have developed are basically the same. That is, they respect the same universal principles which influence the lives of us all. He said that the reason for the serious rise in degenerative illness reflects the general deterioration of our modern society, a society which has grown disrespectful of the traditions of our forbears. Michio speaks in a simple way; his manner is easy and he goes right to the heart of the matter, much as he did during our first meeting when I went to his house to ask him about my cancer and he said to me, "*You* made it, and only *you* can change it." His assessment of me was not only accurate, but it was the perfect thing to say to a woman who had lived her life responding to and thriving on challenge.

Michio talked a lot about families. His theory is that since our families are falling apart as a matter of course, this leads to the breakdown of our communities and eventually to the degeneration of our health. He explained it as if it were a natural progression. I believe this. Ours has always been a close family. We look out for one another despite our differences. That caring has helped us through the times when we've had little money, when our children were doing things we didn't agree with, and when I was sick and needed the love and support of my family. If we feel alone in the world, we appear out of touch and begin to think that we do not matter, but if we are an essential part of something which we consider important, like a family, we are secure in a place in the world. As parents divorce, children run away, and teen-agers cope with multiple sets of real, step, and other parents, we furiously pretend that we belong to a club or fashion or other group, but in fact, underneath it all, there is a dreadful sense of loss. Who are we—where did we come from—where are we going? Michio told us the family is a microcosm. If this

is true, the sense of loss we feel is very real, for when we
lose the essence of belonging to a family, we have indeed lost
a great deal.

Coming from a clinical background, I was fascinated to
learn the things put forward in our oriental "diagnosis" class.
The forms of diagnosis I was familiar with included x-ray,
blood analysis, and other mechanical tests. I was eager to
learn more about the techniques originating in the orient
which enable a person to see the internal condition of someone's body by observing outward physical attributes. I was
very interested to know the techniques which had helped
Michio, Bill Tims, and Bo-In Lee to assess my problem and
to help me. We had a lot of fun in these classes, diagnosing
each other and making jokes about it, but we also learned to
be very careful of the serious aspects of this study. It is a
tool which enables people to help one another. It could, however, be used maliciously or in an insensitive way. We didn't
want to misuse the simple abilities we were learning, yet it
was tempting to try to figure out what was wrong with people
we passed on the street or with people we knew. I know I
would sometimes look at Mama, noticing her nose or her
forehead or some other detail, then catch myself, realizing
I didn't know enough to be doing that.

Dr. Marc Van Cauwenberghe, our instructor for the course
in the macrobiotic approach to healing, had dark hair and was
very slender. He had been in practice as a conventional medical
doctor, I learned, until he too had grown discouraged with
the incompleteness of that approach to health, and had then
discovered and thoroughly absorbed the macrobiotic approach.
As he lectured to us, Marc moved about the room as if he
were in pursuit of tiny, microscopic cancer cells. He would
pick a point out of the air, snatch it up, examine it, then pass
it on to us. "Western medicine," he said, "considers most
cancers to be deadly. The statistics we read about which show
lowered rates in deaths from cancer are due in large part to

the increased ability to deal with *skin* cancer." He scratched
his head and smiled at us. "But this is very misleading, because the statistics show a reduction only of the number and
severity of *symptoms*. Nothing is actually being *cured*," he
emphasized. "What we are usually talking about in modern
medicine is treatment, leading to a reduction in the number
and/or severity of the symptoms."

We were listening intently and he continued. "In order
for a person to totally heal himself, he must engage in serious
reflection about what caused his cancer. He must then change
the diet to include those foods which have been eaten for
thousands of years," he raised his arms to include a vast
space, "and which have *only recently* been ignored as ideal,
daily human nourishment. I speak of macrobiotics."

In his characteristically brusque manner, he had welcomed
us to study medicine from the macrobiotic point of view. I
was to realize that this "medicine" is a synthesis of different
cultures, philosophies, and healing practices spanning the far-
reaching experiences of all of mankind.

I would often think about what we had discussed during
class as I made the forty-minute drive back to Mama's house
in Reading each night. Most often I became absorbed in the
ideas we exchanged in philosophy class, perhaps because this
was the subject with which I was most familiar and to which
I could relate most easily. We spoke of many things which
I had felt inside of me for a long time. I also realized more
about what had happened to me, as I began to eat well.

Jesus saved so many so-called "incurables" in such apparently miraculous fashion, by using commonsense means,
through prayer and fasting. He showed people how to heal
their spirits. Although more difficult than treating symptomat-
ically as does our modern medicine, it is far more fundamental,
working as it does from the inside out. In effect, the person
himself causes the cure. Prayer and fasting are the basic
teachings in all the great religions, not just in Christianity.

Nowadays there is more confidence in medications than there is in the power of our own selves.

Of course, it is much easier to say simply, "I have no control over this illness or this problem. It is simply happening *to* me, and I have no influence on it." Taking it one step further, we then lament, "Why has this awful thing happened to me?" As if to say why didn't it happen to someone else? In my case, I recognize that my cancer didn't befall me. I *did* make it, and truly, in my heart, I wanted to undo what I had done.

* * *

One day, late in October, Michio came to the Erewhon warehouse to chat with the people who worked there. This was something he did regularly.

When it came my turn, I went into the little room used for the purpose and sat down. We talked about my job there at the warehouse, and we talked about the courses I was taking at the Kushi Institute. He asked me about my family and I asked about his. He smiled at me and I smiled back. He asked me how I was feeling and I said I was feeling fine.

Then he told me it seemed as if I had recovered my health.

I can't describe how I felt when he told me. I was very happy, of course. I was ecstatic, proud, relieved. And I knew, inside myself, that what Michio said was true. He didn't really have to tell me. I already knew, somewhere way inside, that I was all better. He was just confirming what, if I thought about it, I already knew. And it was all so *normal*. I got up, shook his hand, thanked him, and went back to work. It was all such a natural part of life.

Back in the office I told the two girls I worked with what Michio had said. They hugged me and we danced around the little room for a few minutes. Then everything was back to normal, and it was just another day. After all, I wasn't any different than I had been an hour before—if I was fully recovered now, I was then, also.

I hoped that my own experience would become part of the experience of the girls in the office and the other people with whom I had come in contact. I hoped they would pass it on to someone else who might need to know about macrobiotics, or that they would use it themselves. This is my reason for writing this book. I want people to have the opportunity to know my story and to see that there is a more comprehensive way of approaching serious illness, to change the horror of a cancer diagnosis into a reaffirmation of a long and fulfilling life.

The weekend following my meeting with Michio at the warehouse I went up to Vermont, where Frank and I stayed with Dexter and Mary at their home in Bridport. We took a day trip to Woodstock, where we had lived for twenty years while we raised our young family. *Twenty years*, I thought as we drove down the well-kept and so-familiar main road through Woodstock. Most people come to this town and spend twenty *minutes*, just passing through, looking at the sights. After all, it is a famous town. The guidebooks describe it as historical, wealthy, and picturesque. I laughed as I remembered how Melissa felt about the hundreds of "leaf-peepers" who came to town each fall to gape at the foliage. "I'd like to see them during mud season," Mel used to snort when the traffic in town became unbearable in late September when the leaves were at their peak. "Getting their cars stuck and their new boots all muddy!" Mel has an eye for comic detail. Underneath our protests we kind of enjoyed the mad crunch right before winter closed us off from the outside world.

Frank had to see someone in town about something having to do with Kingsland Bay. I wandered around the familiar streets while he did his business. I remembered the times we had walked by these stores—not necessarily the same stores, but the same type. I had sometimes wondered if our children were bothered by the fact that we never shopped here in town.

We had always shopped elsewhere where things were less expensive. Our children went to the same school as the wealthy children in town which was probably a good thing so they didn't grow up thinking that the world is filled with people just like ourselves. I hope they felt they had everything they needed.

Looking back, I wonder what we would have done without our good neighbors the Richardsons, especially during the early years when we were just starting out. They were always giving us vegetables and maple syrup, milk from their cows. Steady and reliable, their farm yielded everything they needed and a little more, which they gave to us.

It was months after we arrived on our land here, back in 1959, that we got to know these fine neighbors. Frank was building our first house on the land. One day he looked up and saw two tall boys watching him from a far distance. They stood there for a very long time, Frank told me later on that day. They had stood still for hours, watching him. They came back the next day and did the very same thing. This went on for days, and then one day Frank raised his hand in greeting and they returned the gesture. They moved a little closer each day until finally Frank could see that they were brothers. It seemed that, by the time they were close enough to carry an easy conversation, these quiet, sturdy boys had learned how to build a house, as a result of having watched Frank. Having known city children all our lives, Frank and I were fascinated by this simple, unhurried approach.

I sat down in front of the Woodstock Inn now, a few years since we had left the Woodstock area, and turned my face into the bright, early morning sun. The warmth felt so good I could *smell* it. Suddenly it struck me that during all the years we'd lived on the outskirts of this town I had never, not even once, not while I was walking through the town with the children, a baby in my arms and children holding my hands, running up ahead and falling behind, nor when the children were older and we'd window shop, never once had I stopped as I did today in front of the Woodstock Inn to simply admire the day, the town, to appreciate my life as it was then.

Something in me had truly changed. That place inside me which Michio had awakened during my first visit to see him was finally changing. Frank rounded the corner and I waited for him to come to the bench where I sat in front of the inn.

"Nice day," he said.

"Perfect," I answered. We could have been strangers, so polite were we in our tone, trying to maintain distance with our past and wondering where the future would take us now that our home was no longer here in Woodstock, now that our home was in our hearts.

Later, we drove up the winding backroad to the hundreds of acres of land that had once been ours. It was the same dirt road that Mr. Bumps had struggled down, with me heavy in his arms as Melissa waited, as patiently as she could, to be born. We passed the first house that Frank had built, the one the Richardson boys had watched him build. Then we turned down the narrower dirt road and went by three other houses Frank had built for us. The white one was now yellow; the present owners had cut down the forest in front of the last house we had lived in. We passed the pond that Frank had made. It all seemed strangely long ago, Melissa riding her horse and shouting to me through the kitchen window sounded like an echo to me now.

Frank stopped by the overgrown patch where the barn used to be. We never did figure out what caused the fire. We just got up one morning, and the barn was down on the ground, like socks that have fallen down around your ankles. In a gentle heap it lay there, charred and useless. I know Frank thinks about this when he thinks of Kingsland Bay. Sometimes you just can't figure out why things have happened the way they have. You do the best you can, I guess, to pull up your socks and keep walking.

"Just think," I said, "I might never have come back here again." Frank turned his attention to me. "I might not have wanted to come back," I said. "There wasn't much of anything I really wanted to do back when I was sick."

Frank waited a moment and then asked, "What would you like to do now, Jinny?" He was asking me a big question.

"Well," I said, "I don't know. But right now I'd like to go and see the Richardsons." I thought of something Frank often said, that life is made up of long strings of small events. I think he was relieved we didn't have to decide, that afternoon, against a backdrop of all our former failures and successes, what to do with the rest of our lives.

They weren't expecting us when we drove up the road to their farm. Floyd was on their tractor and Vanita was on the porch making cider. She waved, like always, as if there hadn't been any break in our relationship, as if I hadn't been dying the last time she saw me. The ways of nature did not surprise these people. She came over as I got out of the car, and we embraced, I felt her large, strong body and was comforted. Frank and Floyd shook hands.

"You look . . . good," Floyd said to Frank in his characteristically slow tone.

I had written to them during the summer and told them we hoped to get down to see them in the fall. But Vanita said anyway, "We were wondering when we'd see you."

I looked over their farm which had already turned from rich green to the muted colors of autumn, and knew that we had stayed away too long. My gaze fell on the piles of shiny metal buckets gleaming in the sun. I remembered when we had helped them make their sugar house.

"We took in a lot of syrup this year," Vanita said, then stood back and crossed her arms in front of her with a happy smile. I saw Floyd smiling out of the corner of my eye. You had to know he was smiling, though, because his mouth didn't change. It was more the movement of his eyes that told you he was happy about something.

"Come in and taste," Vanita said.

Their house was filled with the necessities for getting along
in New England. First and foremost were the refrigerators
to keep food for the winter, and then the great wooden shelves
to hold pickled and preserved foods. There was a bed and an
extra small room off to the left. It was clear as soon as you
walked into this house where the owners' priorities lay.
Vanita gave me a taste of the syrup. "Mmmmm," I could feel
the sweet taste rising up out of me.

"Can you have this?" she asked me.

"No," I said, "not really."

Frank went back outside with Floyd. I could see out the
window that Floyd was motioning to Frank about the big oak
tree far off to the left. I could see that the tree was dying.
Vanita and I talked about our children. Then she asked about
me. I told her I was fine, I just *knew* it.

She asked me if a doctor had told me I was okay. I told
her I hadn't seen a doctor, but that I just knew, inside, that
all was well.

She looked at me as if she could accept this very easily,
as if whatever I did she could understand. These Vermonters
were tough to get to know at first, but once you got through
to them they were yours forever. She got up and went to one
of the refrigerators. "For you." She handed me a jar of one of
my favorite foods on earth—her special homemade apple cider
jelly, made from their sweet apple tree. I took the lid off and
stuck my finger into the soft spread. I pulled my finger out
and licked it. Now this, was worth living for.

On Sunday, as always, I was reluctant to leave the family
in Vermont. I felt wistful as I backed out of the driveway and
said my last good-bye to Frank until next weekend. I was off
to a late start and got to my mother's house about midnight.
I was very tired the next morning when I got up at 5 : 30.
Mama put tea on for me and told me I looked tired.

I worked all week and went to class every night. In between, I was still cooking dinner. That next Friday I went

back up to Vermont, and Frank and I stayed with Marion and Fred, his sister and brother-in-law who had had the Christmas party the previous November. It was nearly time for this year's party.

I got in late on Friday night, after class. Frank was waiting up for me, but everyone else in the house was already asleep.

The next morning, laid out on their beautiful dining room table were oatmeal (nothing added, Marion assured me) and freshly made applesauce. The others had their usual breakfast.

"Don't you want anything on that oatmeal?" Fred asked me. Marion stopped on her way back to the kitchen and twisted her hands, listening.

"No, no," I said, holding up my hand. "It's delicious the way it is. You should try it like this," I suggested. "I bet you'd like it." I turned to Marion. "This applesauce is *delicious*."

She turned her small gray head to me. "It's from that tree out there." She pointed through the paned window to a small tree at the back of the house. "I don't know why," she drifted off, "but the apples from that tree are the sweetest of any on our land."

"It's because it's closest to the house and it can see in, while we enjoy eating the apples," Nancy, their younger daughter, said in her whimsical way. She has a delicate way of curling her hair around her finger as she speaks.

Her sister Penny looked up at her as if she were used to her sister's lyrical comments. She, herself, would have said something like, "Well, some trees bear apples that taste sweet and some don't, there's no figuring it." I tried to picture the girls in forty years, when they were my age.

The four women sat drinking coffee for a while (actually three women were drinking, one was watching enviously), and Frank and Fred went outside.

"I've been thinking about this diet of yours," Marion said. "It makes a lot of sense, at least on the surface."

"I've been wondering where certain things come from,

though," Nancy said, "like calcium and B$_{12}$."

I looked down at my now-empty plate. I pointed to it and, running my fingertip over its empty, glossy surface, I said: "Look here, you divide your plate like a pie. First you put a whole grain over here, like so," I said, covering a major portion of the plate with my hand. "Then," I continued, "You put your vegetables from your garden over here—your squash, onions, broccoli, mustard greens, you know." I indicated another, smaller portion of the plate. "And then, your beans and sea vegetables." I pointed to the small, remaining space on the plate. "And there you have a balanced meal. You don't have to worry about calcium or iron or B-vitamins, or anything. It's all right there because you're eating whole foods. It's when you do something to those foods—when you mill them, peel them, or process them in any way, that you start breaking them down and start creating deficiencies. Then you have to start thinking about vitamins and minerals because they are no longer there naturally.

"But how do you know that?" Nancy asked.

I smiled and thought a moment. How *do* you know something like that? Do you know it by measuring it in a test tube or by feeding it to rats? "You know it because you know it," I said. "It's common sense." She seemed ready to accept this.

Marion had been listening quietly. "It's very reasonable," she said. And then, looking over at the two places vacated by Fred and Frank, she said, "But it's awfully difficult to change what people are used to." Our eyes met at the empty chairs.

"Yes it is," I said. "Most people need a *very* good reason to even *think* about what they are eating."

10

We shall not cease from exploration,
And the end of all our exploring
Will be to arrive where we started
And know the place for the first time.
                                    —T. S. Eliot

AFTER MANY WEEKS OF WORKING AT EREWHON, going to
school at night, and spending weekends in Vermont,
I began to show signs of weariness. Then, one morning soon after I had seen Michio at the warehouse, I awakened
feeling very strange. My head was heavy and hot, and I had
a tight feeling in my bladder. When I turned over in bed to
get up, the tight feeling turned to sharp pain. I got up and
walked to the bathroom, hoping to relieve the pressure by
urinating. I was doubled over, with my arms across my lower
body. I passed my mother in the hall.

"Jinny!" she said. "Whatever . . . ." I ran to the bathroom.
The burning passage of urine made me realize I had cystitis.

"Jinny . . . are you all right?" Mama asked on the other
side of the door.

"Yes," I said softly.

"Jinny?" She must not have heard me. "Are you all right?"

I answered again and heard her walk away from the door.
I sat with my head on my fist, leaning on my knee, staring
at the shower curtain.

When I finally got up and looked in the mirror, I was pale
and flushed at the same time, as if I'd been slapped in the face.

I went back to my room and lay down. Soon Mama came
in. I was rolled up in a ball with my arms around my legs.

She sat down on the bed next to me and put her hand on my forehead.

"I'm sure it'll pass," I said. "I was up late last night talking to Tarny, and we drank a lot of tea." I asked Mama to call the warehouse and say I wouldn't be in today.

She paused in the doorway as she left. "Are you sure it's nothing?" She waited. "Are you sure it's nothing we should call a doctor about?"

"No, Mama," I said, "everything's fine. I'm going to sleep for a while now."

I did sleep, off and on, getting up a couple of times to go to the bathroom. The pain was just as bad when I woke up a couple of hours later, and I was still feverish. Mama was sitting on the other bed in the room, watching me.

"Jinny," she said as soon as I opened my eyes, "I don't like the way you look. Not one bit." She leaned forward. "I think we should call a doctor."

I sat up and tried to figure out how I felt.

"Jinny," she said, "are you listening?"

"Yes, I heard you," I said. "I just . . . give me a minute, Mama, will you? Just one little minute?" I fell back onto the pillows. I really felt awful. Mama left the room and I went back to sleep.

When I woke up again it was dark. I felt a little better and decided to get up. The house was quiet, and I felt soothed and a little relieved. The pain was still there, though. I went into the bathroom and put cold water on my face. I still looked terrible. I heard voices in the kitchen. I put some lipstick on and went to the kitchen to make myself something to eat. Then I had the overwhelming urge to urinate and had to turn back for the bathroom. Once there, nothing came of it. "Goodness," I thought, "what next?" I looked around the tiny pink bathroom and thought, "Will I be spending the rest of my life in here or what?" I could see the newspaper headlines now, *Woman, 60, Recovers From Cancer and Spends Rest of Life in Tiny Pink Bathroom at Mother's House.* Not funny.

Mama and Tarny were talking at the kitchen table when I came into the room.

"Jinny, sit down, will you?" Tarny asked.

"No, thanks," I answered. "I want to make something to eat. Besides, I'm more comfortable standing." I went to the refrigerator for an onion to make some miso soup. This will straighten me out, I thought, if I can only resist the need to run to the bathroom when I put water in the pan.

"Jinny," Mama began, "we're very worried about you. I think you should see a doctor. You need some medication for this." Her voice changed. "I remember when you were a little girl, you used to get something like this. It would go on for days if you didn't take your medicine. And you're already so weak, dear . . . ." She was referring to the fact that I was still very thin.

I peeled the onion and sliced it into thin rounds. Then I went back to the refrigerator for a carrot.

"Jinny, you need more than an onion and a carrot for cystitis," my sister said, putting her entire being behind her remark. "Good Heavens," she said, "why don't you take a little help?"

I turned around with the knife in my hand, motioning to her with it. "I've got to do it my way," I said.

The phone rang and Mama left the room to answer it.

"Jinny," Tarny said, "I know you'll do what you want, but won't you think of Mama just a little? She's worried sick." She peered into my face with her huge brown eyes. "What's the harm in just seeing a doctor? He doesn't have to *do* anything."

Then I put the lid on the pot and put it on the stove. I took the miso out of the cabinet, off the shelf which held all my other food staples—tamari, brown rice, azuki beans, millet, etc.—my sustenance, my well being, my salvation, my medicine cabinet. All I had to do was figure out what combinations of these ingredients to use to feel better. I knew the answer was right there on that shelf, but I just didn't know how to go about it.

"I know what I'm doing," I said finally. "I really do." And then I added, "Let's not fight, okay?"

"I'm not fighting, Jinny," she said. "I just really care about what happens to you. You take it the wrong way."

I sat down with my bowl of soup and began to eat. I looked out the window and noticed for the first time that it had been snowing all day. There were about five inches of snow on the ground. "I hope this snow stops," Mama said as she came back into the room. "I don't know what we'll do if we have to go anywhere in a hurry." She looked at me.

"We aren't going to have to go anywhere in a hurry, Mama," I said, and continued to eat.

"How's that going down?" she asked me.

"Fine," I said.

Mama didn't say any more about doctors that evening, but I could tell she was still worried about me. I leaned over her chair and kissed her goodnight.

I was up and down all night, feverish and in pain.

Early the next morning Mama knocked softly at my door. I pretended I was asleep and didn't answer. I felt I didn't quite have myself collected yet to face the day. I lay there thinking about what I'd been eating. Everything was according to my diet. I had been sure I'd be better when I woke up this morning, but I was mistaken. The pain was still there and I was still feverish.

From my nursing experience I knew that cystitis is an infection in the bladder. But what, considering how well I was eating, would cause this infection? Then I thought about what we had been studying at the Kushi Institute. We had learned basic principles of harmony and balance. Illness is caused by a disharmony or lack of balance, but I couldn't figure out what it was, in my case.

I got up, dressed, and called Bill Tims. I told him my symptoms. He agreed with my diagnosis of cystitis. He told me to grate a fresh sour apple and eat that two or three times a day until I felt better. He explained that he thought I had become "too tight," a kind of mild imbalance from eating strictly for over a year, and this might he helpful in my particular situation.

I went off to the kitchen to prepare the apple. Mama followed.

"What are you going to do with the apples, Jinny?" she asked. This, I knew rather than irritating Mama, would fascinate her.

"Have you got a grater?" I asked her.

She took one from the drawer by the sink. I grated one of the apples and put it in a dish.

"Now what?" she asked.

"Now I eat it," I replied.

"That's it?" she asked.

"That's it," I said. We both smiled, and I sat down at the table next to her. She watched me eat the apple.

When I had finished, she asked, "So that's it?"

"Yup," I answered, "that's it."

"How long does it take?" Mama asked.

"Don't know," I said. "We'll see."

"Do you eat this again?" she asked.

"Yes, in a few hours," I told her. And then, "Excuse me, I have to go . . . ." I felt as though I hadn't urinated in six months.

Mama sighed as I left the room.

A couple of hours later I grated another apple and ate it. I was feeling a bit better. I didn't feel quite so hot. I noticed, however, that Mama was looking very pale. The fact that I was noticing what was going on around me made me realize I was feeling a little bit better.

Tarny came over that afternoon. She brewed coffee and sat with Mama. They were talking about the snow.

Later I called David, and he told me to come home right

away. Mama insisted on going with me back to Vermont. So
the next morning I put her in the car and drove us to David
and Deborah's. The roads were beautiful; crisp with fresh
snow, the trees were hanging over the back streets near my
mother's house like jewelry trees holding dangling necklaces
of ice. Everything was glistening in the sun.

Driving north on Route 89, I could feel that I was no longer
in control. I pulled a towel from my bag and shoved it under
me. There was no pride now. I just wanted to get home.

Dave, Deb, and Frank said they'd be there waiting for me
when I got there. I focused my mind on an image of them
standing in the doorway of the house, looking out, waiting
for me to drive into the driveway. I kept that mental picture
in front of me the whole way home. It's what kept me from
pulling over to the side of the road and crying, many times
along the way.

The day was clear and bright and new with snow. I had
traveled this route so many times during the last couple of
months, during the last twenty years. Today, however, I saw
very little of it. It seemed as though I were driving at night.
I was hardly aware of Mama sitting beside me.

When we got to David and Deb's house, David was standing in the doorway, just as I'd imagined. He came out to the
car as we drove up. Deborah came to the doorway with a
dishtowel in her hands. Frank dashed by her and came out to
the car. He kissed me and helped me out of the car.

"I'm afraid I . . . ." I wanted to explain about the towel
and my skirt being wet. Deborah took my other arm, and we
walked into the house. David helped Mama out of the car and
inside.

David told Deb to draw a warm bath for me. She took my
soggy clothes and helped me into the water. I heard them
talking outside the door to the bathroom. I heard them say
the word "discharge." I heard them say it twice, maybe three
times. I slid down further in the tub and let the warm water
run over me. I had heard that word, "discharge," before in

one of our classes at the institute. It seems it stood for "getting better."

David put me to bed, with a big Turkish towel under me. "This is a traditional home care plaster," he said, as he rolled me over and placed it on my skin over the area where my kidneys are. Deborah came into the room. I reached out for her hand and said, "If I'd known I was going to be such a mess, I wouldn't have come."

"Well, really, Mother," she arched her eyebrows at me and winked, "if we'd known what a mess you were, we wouldn't have invited you."

David grunted and left the room.

A few minutes later he returned with a fresh plaster.

"How long do I stay like this?" I asked him.

"Another fifteen minutes," he answered.

"What is this supposed to do?" I asked.

He said my kidneys were constricted and it would help them to relax.

"Thank you," I said.

"You're welcome," he answered.

My fever stayed very high for four days, way up around 104 degrees. Then, gradually it started to come down. I lay on the couch in the living room barely awake most of the time. I remember my granddaughter Jessica reaching for my hand, holding it with her tiny fingers, silently, softly stroking my skin, sometimes whispering "Grammy," as softly as she could.

"I'm fine, Frank, really," I told him. He looked as upset as he had when I had told him I had malignant melanoma, stage IV. "It's the last hurrah," I said.

David turned around. "That's exactly what it is. I can't believe you see that."

"I *have* learned *something*, you know. I'm not nearly so dumb as I was a year ago, David," I waved a limp hand at him.

"You mean this cystitis has something to do with your

cancer?" Frank asked.

"I think it's the cancer's last breath." I smiled and turned my head to face the inside of the couch. I was pleased with the way I had said that because it was exactly how I felt. My cancer had had the life squeezed out of it.

Mama was frantic with worry, as my fever stayed high, and tried in vain to convince us to call a doctor. She was so upset Frank asked her if she wanted to go home. Finally, he did take her back. Dave and Deb continued giving me plasters and sitting up with me all night. Finally, on the fourth or fifth day the fever broke and I sat up, looking for something to eat.

* * *

I didn't go back to Boston after that. It would have been too much. Frank arranged for us to stay in a beautiful house near Deb and Dave's that belonged to a young friend of ours. We lived in the house in exchange for the repairwork we had agreed to do on the house. The time we spent there was very special for Frank and me, and we often look back with a lot of appreciation for the days we lived in that house in the beautiful winter countryside.

We lived very naturally that winter and spring. Frank cut firewood which we used to stoke the woodstove to heat the house and cook our food. I meditated each morning under the shadow of a big, beautiful maple tree on a hill. In February we maple-sugared for the first time. We slid down the road on icy days when the children were over, as Frank met us at the bottom of the hill with the truck. It was a simple, carefree time. We were at ease to walk through the woods and watch the sky for hours. It was time alone for Frank and me, time to hold hands and think about ourselves, together.

I felt much stronger at the end of our stay there. I felt truly recovered from all our mishaps of the previous few

years, and ready to get on with our lives. Now that my
strength had returned, I began thinking about how I could
share my experience with other people. It wasn't enough to
simply blend back into the Vermont countryside from whence
I had come. I had learned a lot and wanted to share what I
had to offer. I had thought quite a bit about how best to do
this, had talked a little bit about it with Frank and the children. There were many options.

Soon, I told the family I had decided on a new project, one
which, for the people we would meet, might help to bring
new solutions to old problems.

11

Fear not the night; the morning follows soon.
Each has his task to make the earth more fair.
It is by these, by midnight and by noon,
That she grows riper and her orchards bear.
Her fields would wither in a sun too bright;
They need darkness too. Fear not the night.
— Robert Nathan

W E WERE ALL SITTING around at Dave and Deb's one
night. The fireplace was going. Deb was making
cookies and Jessie was curled up in Frank's lap.
He was staring into the fire. David was by the door shining
his boots and talking to the dog. Geo and Julie and Dexter
and Mary were dotted around the room, draped over old
stuffed chairs, holding hands, talking quietly, making shadows
against the walls in the firelight.

"Do we still have the kitchen things from Kingsland Bay?"
I asked Frank.

"Mmmm Hmmm," Frank answered.

"We do? Are you sure?" I asked again.

"I think so . . . sure . . . , they're in the barn," he said. He
was thinking, looking into the fire. The implications of what
I was asking hadn't hit him.

Deb came in with a plate of warm cookies and set them on
the table. Jessie rolled out of Frank's lap and kneeled on the
floor by the table where her mother had just laid the plate
of cookies.

Frank looked up. "What are you thinking about, Jinny?"
he asked me slowly.

"Well," I said, "I saw the greatest place over in South Royalton . . . it's small, needs some work. It's very reasonable."

"Is someone looking for a place," Frank asked, "or are you just interested in what's going on in real estate in South Royalton?"

"Well, it *is* a nice town, Frank . . ." I said.

"A nice town for what?" he asked.

"For anything," I insisted.

He looked back into the fire.

"Can I have a cookie?" Jessie asked. She was still on the floor, looking at the plate of cookies.

"Okay, Jessie," her father answered her.

Turning back to me, Frank asked, "Did you have anything specific in mind for this place in South Royalton?" I looked at his tired face and thought about not continuing with what I wanted to say. He had dealt with so much during the past two years. After everything that had happened, did I have the right to go on with what I'd planned to say?

I looked at my hands. Jessie finished her cookie and hopped back into Frank's lap. He squeezed her and sighed. She lay very still and the room grew quiet.

"I want to open a health food store in South Royalton," I said softly.

Everyone looked up.

"Shoot, David," Deborah came bounding into the room.

"There's a coon in the shed, and it knocked over a bag of onions. I tripped over the things and hit my . . ." She stopped, rubbing her back and looked at us. "We really have to fix that . . . ." She looked up again. "What's going on here?" she asked finally.

"Mother is going to open a health food store," David answered her. "In South Royalton," he added, setting down the boot he was working on. He got up and stretched his legs. He went over to the fire and poked a log. Frank continued to stare in the direction of the fire, at David's back. Debbie sat down.

Geo shifted in his chair. Julie turned to look at him. Dexter got up and joined David by the fire. He rubbed his hands, then stooped to pick up a twig and throw it back into the fire. Mary bit a piece of skin off her finger.

"I think we should talk about this," Frank said, straightening in his chair. Jessie looked up at him, her hair falling over his knees.

Deb moved over by Mary, David and Dexter turned around, the others looked up.

"I know we don't have the money," I began. Someone gave a low hoot. "I know we're all tired of businesses that don't work." I looked around at them, knowing what they were feeling. "This *will* work, though. It's *got* to."

"Mother and I have talked about this," Deb said. David started at her. "We've talked about it, and *I* think it's a great idea. Mother has a lot to offer people—she always has, but especially now. And besides, I told Mother I'd help her do it."

"We already know how to do everything," I continued. "It wouldn't be difficult. We could just start. It would all come about; I just know it. There isn't that much to do on the inside." Frank looked up. "Just some tables and chairs we'd have to make; shelves, things like that." I hugged my knees and became quiet.

* * *

During the next three months Frank and the boys renovated the shed I had seen in South Royalton. The girls and I did all the electrical work and the painting and decorating. We were all proud at the end of the three months to find that we had made a very attractive natural food store—and we had decided to add a bakery too. Here was another example of what we could all do together.

We placed index cards around on the shelves describing unusual foods. We hung various posters and we often talked with our customers about natural foods.

The bakery ended up doing much more business than the store, as people came to us for freshly baked breads and pies. Soon, we began to make some main dishes, for take-out customers.

Deb and I were doing a lot of the cooking and running the store, while my niece Nancy did the baking. I remember one day three of us were sitting down after a long day. Deb was eating a piece of apple pie. "Well," she said, "I can see I'm going to gain some weight at *this* job."

I ran my eyes over her slim, strong body. "Not likely, dear, not with the running around we're doing."

Frank and David came through the door after they'd finished their work for the day. "Well, this is a happy scene," David said. "Did somebody make some money or something?" He gave Deb a kiss and settled down to eat the rest of the apple pie. Frank brought fresh heated cider from the kitchen.

"Did you have hot cider today, Mother?" David asked me.

"Yup!" I could feel my eyes shining as I looked back at him. I was a woman who had survived cancer to sit here with her family drinking hot apple cider. I loved this.

I bet he had told Deb to keep an eye on what I ate during the day—to make sure I kept away from things I should be careful of. I looked at Deb. She waved her hand as if to say, "Don't worry, we're partners." I really didn't want to eat anything I wasn't supposed to, anyway. It was just the idea that David was still watching me . . . .

"So, you think this is going to work?" David asked, leaning back in his chair, away from the empty pie plate.

"Sure I do," I said. "A lot of good people are depending on it." I was referring to my family, but I also meant all the people I wanted to reach with my experience of dietary and spritual change . . . .

Sometimes we even saw a few people from Boston. One day three young people came in who were studying at the Kushi Institute. I told them I had gone there and I explained a little bit about what I had been through with cancer.

"Ellen here has an ovarian cyst," the young man in the group said. He had a clean, clear face and was obviously in love with Ellen.

"What do you think?" Ellen asked. "Do you think I can get rid of it by eating macrobiotically?"

"It's more important what *you* think," I said.

She looked at me intently. "I see what you mean," she said. "I do doubt it sometimes, but something tells me it really *will* work."

"Then it will," I told her.

Nancy, Deb, and I worked hard at keeping the store and bakery going. It became a very stressful time for us, though, as we realized the business was failing. I was working much too hard and seemed to be falling back into my old ways of not taking care of myself. We were very disappointed when we realized we wouldn't be able to keep the doors to the store open much longer. We had met a lot of people, made many friends and, I hope, influenced some people to take another look at the way they were eating. The truth of the matter is, we weren't making any money.

"It's really hard to close the restaurant," I told Frank one night toward the end, more than a year after we had started. "Especially when people come in with such problems." I told him about a woman I had spoken to that day.

"She was about fifty," I told him, "and she had trouble holding her spoon to eat her soup." I remember how grateful she was when I handed her a cup of pea soup that Deb had just finished making.

Frank looked up from his newspaper. "She's very sick?" he asked.

"Arthritis," I told him. "Bad."

He shook his head. "Did you tell her about macrobiotics?"

"I did. I sat down with her and told her all about it. I told her about what *I* did. She told me she'd had arthritis for fifteen years. Nothing helps. The pain is so bad sometimes, she says she wants to die."

"Is that what she said?" Frank asked.

"Her husband is dead." I was remembering how the tight curls on the woman's head had jiggled around her face as she told me. "And," I added, "her son has cancer."

We sat in silence for a few minutes. Frank folded the newspaper and held it in both hands on his lap. "We're very lucky, Jinny," Frank said, "considering what could have happened."

"Lucky, yes, Frank," I said. "Lucky we could see a way to help ourselves."

"It's so hard to tell people how to see that way," Frank said. "I try to tell people I meet. This one has an ulcer, another one's wife can't have children . . . I don't know, how do you tell people?" He thought a moment. "Why is it that we, or rather that *you* saw what to do?" He looked at me. "You saw so clearly, Jinny—why?"

"I wish I could answer that," I said. "It has something to do with spirit and belief. The desire to live and to really change. I needed to change, Frank. I *desperately* needed to change."

He came over to the chair where I was sitting. "Were things that bad?" he asked. "I mean, were things bad between us?"

"I didn't feel I had any direction," I said. "The children were grown; I felt edgy about not having anything important to do."

"What about the hospital? You always liked that. Didn't you want to go back to that?"

"I was tired of it. Tired of the procedures, the pills, and the therapies and the surgery. Tired—really, really tired, of the people who were dying anyway. They're just not getting *well*, Frank."

He looked at his hands. "I couldn't accept being sick," I said. "I'd known for a long time that something was wrong.

I just went along with it even though I could feel it in my bones, see it when I looked at myself. My face was puffy, I was ugly. I didn't *do* anything about it because I didn't know what to do. I didn't want to lie down on one of those long white hospital beds and turn in response to treatment and then finally, after suffering as much as I could, leave that stuffy building . . . in a bag." I stopped, and then continued. "I just stopped *believing* in it, Frank. I wanted to help people, and I had the feeling I wasn't doing all that was necessary." I put my head in my hands. If I could have laid it in my lap and dissolved in the darkness provided there . . . .

"And that's it," I said suddenly, getting up out of the chair. "Let's see what's for dinner." Debbie had packed up a bag of leftovers from the take-out counter at the store. "Wait until you try this, Frank. Deb made the greatest sweet and sour tofu. "Here," I said, "let's boil some noodles."

"Jinny," Frank said, taking the pot out of my hand. "Let's just eat it cold." He pulled me to the table where we ate out of the carboard container and remembered how we were when we were young.

12

There is so much to be done and
so many who need help . . .
　　　　　　　　—Edgar Cayce

Mother's a celebrity," Frank was on the phone
talking to Julie. "They want her to come to
Boston to speak." Then, "Yeah . . . yeah . . . ."
I couldn't hear the rest. I was putting a few things in an
overnight bag for Frank and me. "Okay, Honey, see you
when we get back," Frank's voice rose to where I could hear
it again. "Bye now . . . ."

We went to Boston where I spoke at a macrobiotic health
seminar similar to the one where Michio spoke to me for the
second time and told me I had improved by about seventy-
five percent. It felt great to tell about what had happened to
me. I felt like Diane Silver or any of the others I had seen at
Amherst three years before. I was talking about my cancer
in the past tense. I looked at Frank in the audience and thought,
"Thank you, . . . thank you for helping me explore all these
things . . . thank you for being there . . . quiet and sturdy . . .
for me."

"It helps," I told the audience, "if you have a family that
supports what you're doing. This is really essential, along
with your faith and conviction that you will get well."

When I explained that my illness had cost our family ap-
proximately $160, everyone was stunned by this relatively
insignificant amount of money. I might also have said that our
weekly food bill was less from then on, as well.

I saw Mr. Kushi at the seminar. He smiled at me and said,

"It goes well?" It was both a question and an affirmation. He was telling me and asking me and helping me to see that it was so. Frank reached over and shook his hand. Michio pressed his mouth together and pumped Frank's hand, nodding all the while.

While at the conference, I heard about a hospital in the Boston area that was planning to study the effects of the macrobiotic diet on some of its patients. They also were beginning to serve macrobiotic meals to their staff. Perhaps this would be a way for me to go back to nursing and blend my past experience with the new things I had learned.

I decided to apply to this hospital, the Lemuel Shattuck Hospital in Jamaica Plain, Massachusetts. The application procedure required that I have a complete physical examination given by their staff.

I told the doctors at the Shattuck Hospital that I had been diagnosed as having had cancer in 1978. They gave me a through examination and found no traces of the disease. They told me I had the job. This was in April of 1982, nearly four years after I was diagnosed as having malignant melanoma, stage IV. Where would I have been had I taken the doctor's advice four years ago? I believe that the rigors of the treatments that were recommended to me at that time would try the vitality of a healthy person, let alone a very sick one. I don't think I would have lived through it.

I moved to Boston in April and stayed with my mother again. Things were different this time. I was stronger and looked better than I had in years. I had gained weight and the color in my face was very natural. I had much more energy and Mama and I had fun joking over my food. "Nuts and bolts," she called macrobiotic food. Maybe she meant that it is "basic" food, or maybe she found it hard to chew after years of white bread and processed food.

I talked to her a little bit about my feelings about the failure of our store in South Royalton. I told her we weren't sorry about the effort we had put into it. It wasn't wasted

because we had talked to many people and, hopefully, we had
made an impression. It was frustrating, though, to have this
great thing, macrobiotics, and no way of spilling it out. I told
her, "You can't just stop people on the street and say, 'Hey,
look what happened to me; maybe you could use this information, or your mother, or your brother, or your friend.' "
Mama looked at me as if she were going to ask me if that
was what I had in mind to do.

"No, Mama," I reassured her, "I'm not going to run
around like a fool, but only because it wouldn't work. If
people would listen, I wouldn't mind looking a little crazy."

Working at the Shattuck is a more practical way of reaching people. I can work together with medical professionals in
a world that is very familiar to me and, perhaps, have some
influence there in view of my experience with macrobiotics.
It would have been difficult for me to simply go back to an
ordinary hospital, but since the Shattuck was interested in
investigating the link between diet and disease, it seemed like
a terrific opportunity to be useful at this juncture.

I became the head nurse on the geriatric mental ward of
the hospital. This is a security ward which treats mentally
ill adults who have been institutionalized for most of their
lives. The hospital, in conjunction with Tufts University, did
a study on my ward to test the effects of the macrobiotic diet.
Ten patients on my ward were fed macrobiotic meals—no
meat or dairy foods, eggs, sugar, white bread, etc. Instead
they were given brown rice, fresh vegetables, beans, sea
vegetables, and the rest. After two weeks of eating this way
many of the patients showed improvements. One woman who
hadn't been able to feed herself in many years began to feed
herself. Another patient got out of bed one day and walked
to the nurse's station. She hadn't done anything like that in
many years. Many of the patients who previously could not
make eye contact with the nurses, began to do so.

Then the study ended and the food trays came back on the
floor filled with white bread, jello, meat, and canned vege-

tables. Everything went back to the way it had been before the study began. The patients went back the way they had been before the change in diet. There is some talk that this study will be resumed. I hope so.

I appreciate the fact that the Shattuck Hospital is open to the principles of macrobiotics, continuing to provide wholesome lunches for the staff and encouraging members of the nearby East West Foundation to come and speak to the staff of the hospital. I hope the orthodox medical community and the alternative medical community will always keep the door open between them. There is a lot to be done, and we can do a better job if we all work together.

I really enjoy working at the Shattuck. My staff and secretary are wonderful. I'm so fortunate to be working with such giving, caring people.

* * *

Frank moved to Boston that December and we rented a small apartment near where I had lived when I was doing my nurse's training thirty-five years ago. From it, we can hear the ambulance sirens during the night, as I did so long ago. Their sound is different now; a higher, more modern sound, but the import of that insistent, fast-moving sound has not changed. Still, I try to visualize the person inside the van—still I wonder, could I help?

Also from our window, we can see the Charles River. Every day Frank and I walk along its banks. So many things to see —different from being in the country. There are people on rollerskates everywhere with dogs, babies, children. We saw an old priest take his shoes off in June and walk on the grass. Everywhere people are making music, laughing, walking, running . . . . We like to stop on the stone bridges and watch the baby ducks in the spring. "They're a lot like us," I told Frank. "They each go off, but always they slide back together again." We watched them glide away, then pull back to the fold.

Since being in Boston I have had more opportunity to become involved in seminars sponsored by the East West Foundation. Some days I will work eight hours at the hospital, and then that evening I will talk with people who have come to the Foundation to find out more about improving their health.

One thing strikes me about people who are this sick, regardless of whether they are in a hospital or they are looking for an alternative; they are all very scared. When they see someone such as me, standing up and telling them, "This is what happened to me and this is what I'm doing now, six years later," they seem to relax a little. They seem to understand that they, too, can make it happen—that they can make a miracle for themselves; not a miracle bestowed upon us only by God or by an outside force. Every day each of us can make for ourselves a little miracle.

It's easy to become sentimental, to become dramatic about our lives. We want to *destroy* cancer cells and *fight* leukemia. We get caught up in the extremes of life, and we forget to appreciate each moment. Outwardly we bemoan our misfortunes and those of others. We are more comfortable doing this than we are facing the mess inside ourselves. We don't need to continue to clutter our lives with old ways. We need to clean house.

Frank has work in Boston now. We are paying off our debts, left over from Kingsland Bay and the store. I love being in the city after twenty-five years in Vermont. Our children come down to visit often, or we go up there. Our whole family is still in Vermont—sons, daughters, grandchildren, friends; everyone except Judith, who lives in San Francisco. We are all macrobiotic. David still worries about me. They still bring onions and fresh kale from their garden. He peers over my shoulder in our tiny, city apartment kitchen and tells me, "Watch those onions! Don't let them burn!"

He says that city living is unhealthy, that we're taking a *big risk* living in the city. All I know is, *I really love it!* And that's at least as important as eating right!

However, I do think we need people like David to monitor our sloppy ways. Sometimes he has the courage which the rest of us lack. But it's really not necessary to drive yourself crazy over all the details of the macrobiotic diet. It *is* better to be in a good mood when you cook. It *is* better not to burn the food and not to overcook the vegetables. These things, in addition to eating the right foods, are very important, but it's not necessary to become frantic over it. I've seen people become paralyzed with fear that they're going to do something wrong when they cook for someone who has cancer. It is important to be careful, but most of all, plain common sense will do. The most important thing of all is to be surrounded by love and to keep a sense of humor about it all.

Getting well is a process, like life itself. I didn't wake up one morning, suddenly all better. Gradually, the cancer left me, slowly, as it had come.

To be sure, I would rather not be writing this book in a way, for it dredges up a lot of unhappy memories. The time during which I was suffering from cancer was very hard for us in many ways. We would rather forget about it. I want others to know my story, though, if it might be of some help. Please know, if you have a serious illness or if you know someone who does, that *there is a choice*. You can seek an alternative and change the course of your life.

Note to the Reader

Further information on the macrobiotic approach to health can be obtained from The East West Foundation, a non-profit institution established in 1972. The East West Foundation, its seven major affiliates, and regional offices around the country, offer ongoing classes for the general public in macrobiotic cooking and related subjects.

BOSTON HEADQUARTERS:
Macrobiotics International and
The East West Foundation
17 Station St.
Brookline, MA 02147
(617) 731–0564

MARYLAND
4803 Yellowwood Rd.
Baltimore, MD 21209
(301) 367–6655

CALIFORNIA
708 N. Orange Grove Ave.
Hollywood, CA 90046
(213) 651–5491

COLORADO
1931 Mapleton Ave.
Boulder, CO 80302
(303) 449–6754

CONNECTICUT
184 East Main St.
Middletown, CT 06457
(203) 344–0090

ILLINOIS
1574 Asbury Ave.
Evanston, IL 60201
(312) 328–6632

PHILADELPHIA
606 S. Ninth St.
Philadelphia, PA 19147
(215) 922–4567

WASHINGTON, D.C.
Box 40012
Washington, DC 20016
(301) 897–8352